INSIDE TWENTY-FIVE MORE CLASSIC CHILDREN'S STORIES

Discovering Values at Home or in School

by Miriam J. Johnson

Paulist Press
New York and Mahwah

Interior art by Kathy Nevins.

Copyright © 1988
by Miriam Johnson

Library of Congress Cataloging-in-Publication Data

Johnson, Miriam, 1932–
    Inside twenty-five more classic children's stories : discovering
values at home or in school / by Miriam J. Johnson.
        p.   cm.
    ISBN 0-8091-3036-X (pbk.) : $4.95 (est.)
    1. Children's stories—History and criticism.   2. Moral education—
Handbooks, manuals, etc.   3. Religious education of children—
Handbooks, manuals, etc.   I. Title.   II. Title: Inside 25 more
classic children's stories.
PN3347.J594   1989   88-25411
809.3—dc19   CIP

Published by Paulist Press
997 Macarthur Boulevard
Mahwah, New Jersey 07430

Printed and bound in the
United States of America

For my grandson Seth Andrew

Contents

Preface

One of the fascinating aspects of writing is that no single author can say everything there is to say about a subject. In fact, the author is the first person to experience this dynamic that comes with the use of words. He or she can put something on paper one day and upon returning to it see a different way of expressing a thought. Ideas have a way of growing or incubating in the mind. Thoughts expand as if nourished by all the experiences that are stored in a person's memory.

When it comes to stories the plot thickens. Characters rush from one adventure to another with little time to ask why or to reflect on what words or actions mean. However, as I noted in the Preface to *Inside Twenty-Five Classic Children's Stories: Discovering Values at Home or in School*, the reader has ample time to fill in the blank spaces between the lines or words on a page. Indeed, that part of the story can already be present in the mind of the reader so that a kind of dialogue is set up between the reader and the writer concerning what is written.

Isaac Bashevis Singer, in a recent award-winning PBS documentary on his life and work, gave expression to what I am saying when he stated, "The reader can create a message. I don't have to do everything for the reader."

In this statement Singer, the author of a number of children's classics, shows a marvelous understanding of the interaction between writer and reader. He does not feel the need to have the last word. What he writes may be the first word—the springboard that allows the reader to take off on his or her own. He feels no need to control what is meant by his words. He is free and he frees the reader.

I must admit that at first I was uncomfortable with using the word "value" to describe the message I was getting from or giving to the stories in this book. Then it occurred to me that attaching value to such ideals as freedom, equality, or compassion points to a source, and that source is God. To take into account the Giver of the value seemed important here in America where ninety-five percent of the people believe in the existence of God.

In this volume, as in the first one, I am interested in how various

1

authors treat not only values but the Source or Giver of Values. I found that some, such as Robert McCloskey in *Time of Wonder*, refer to that Giver somewhat indirectly, or implicitly. The stars gaze down like "one hundred pair of eyes watching you," he writes, but "one pair of eyes is watching over all." That this points to God is clear since such an ability is one only God possesses. That God's work creates a sense of awe and reverence for nature is perhaps not surprising. This is what gives it value. To ignore this seemed to me to be a tragedy.

I found other stories where the reference to God was explicit. *Are You There God? It's Me, Margaret* has it in the title, whereas in *Bridge to Terabithia* the reference appears in the story. In these books the reference is intended. It is there to be picked up as part of the message.

In still other books the religious values might not be necessarily intended. However, the content of these stories ties in with or parallels something in the Bible so clearly as to suggest a common source of inspiration or value, known or unrealized by the writer. *Yertle the Turtle* is a good example of this, as is *Miss Nelson Is Missing*. The message of equality in Dr. Seuss' book is deeply embedded in the Old Testament prophets and in the ministry of Jesus. And both in structure and in content the change from a smiling, friendly Miss Nelson to the stern Miss Swamp turn the biblical concept of law and gospel into a kind of parable.

I found that in thinking about values and their Source, the selected stories fell into four groups and naming them followed rather easily. The title of the first section, "A Design in Nature," became apparent in the stories that focus on death, human differences, or the value of time. However, there is nothing we humans have or use that has not been made for a purpose. We have designed everything that we own or make use of. And just as in our own "things" there is no design without the human designer, so also in relation to what we as humans have not invented or manufactured there is no design without a Designer. Sometimes the connection is an active one suggesting some kind of intervention as with hurricanes and hummingbirds. At other times the connection is a passive one, as if built-in. Either way, as a design it is observable and I feel it is necessary to include the Source as we think about the value of gratitude, or truth, or awe and mystery.

In each of the stories grouped in Section Two, a situation is redeemed, and the moment one speaks of redemption one thinks of a redeemer, either on a human scale, or in relation to God. The very idea of redemption which describes what happens in these stories is indebted to the biblical story. Again the value is one of gratitude or truth, or, in literary terms, giving credit to the source.

The stories in Section Three also have their own common bond. They all connect with the poor. And the motif of social or economic justice is so strong, so obviously reflective of biblical background, that the theological overtone in these stories will seem like a natural connection to many readers. For those who would like additional rationale, they can perhaps find it in the thinking of Carl Braaten, a Lutheran theologian, who wrote in *The Future of God* (New York: Harper & Row, 1969, p. 95): "God is the hidden pressure for justice at work in the world." While there is biblical precedent for relating God and justice, we do not directly or immediately perceive God's activity within us or among us. God's presence is hidden as it were. The value we place in America on "liberty and justice for all" is one the "founding fathers" and mothers related without reservation to the Creator.

The last section grew out of the common bond of love that these stories have. It emerged in ordinary settings as in *Sarah, Plain and Tall* or in extraordinary ones as in *The Whipping Boy*. It appeared in a home, a department store, in the country, and in the family of a minister and of a ruler. While the settings differed, the dynamic of love is present in diverse ways. Hence, love is a value that might be regarded as a "many splendored thing." Identifying God as involved in human love was done because "God is love" (1 John 4:16) and "in God we live and move and have our being" (Acts 17:28).

In conclusion, I would like to give some words of explanation as to how I feel this book can enable readers to "get inside" some of these twenty-five classic children's stories. I can envision parents, teachers, and pastors reading the descriptions and interpretations of the various stories and deciding which books are age appropriate and of interest to the children with whom they share books. Some stories are very short and may seem appropriate for only the youngest of children. However, these books contain some profound insights into contemporary issues and concerns with which older children are struggling. Therefore in this book it is misleading to label stories by age level. Parents might think through what concepts and Conversation Starters they feel would be the most relevant and interesting to talk about in a casual and succinct way. Generally the Conversation Starters are arranged so that the less difficult ones come first.

This book is not intended to be read to children or to encourage long, drawn-out discussions with a moralizing tone. Children's books are, first and foremost, to be enjoyed. Talking about the meanings and the values hidden or explicit in the stories presented here (which ought to be available at most libraries) can add to that enjoyment and enhance the time adults and children spend together with books.

A Design in Nature

Hurricanes and Hummingbirds

TIME OF WONDER
by Robert McCloskey
63 pages
(New York: Viking, 1957)

> *People and the rest of created life become one when nature's fury attacks a small town along the coast of Maine. It raises the haunting question though, "Where do hummingbirds go in a hurricane?"*

Along the coast of Maine there are many tiny islands on which people live, some all year round, many just during the summer. Like a prelude to a concert the author shows in picture and words a small cloud approaching, bringing with it dark shadows and rain causing a million splashes. There is both anxiety and awe for those who inhabit the tiny islands.

Spring, Summer, and Fall are the times of wonder Robert McCloskey presents, each with its own theme, its own melody, its own surprises.

There is a certain serenity to Spring along the coast. So small are the coves amidst the islands that a lobster fisherman who goes out to pull up his traps sets off ripples from his boat which strike the nearest shore first and then as an echo in a cave one can hear them land on the opposite shore.

At times nature is so quiet you can hear the ferns grow, pushing aside dead leaves and poking their heads upward.

Fog is a common visitor to these islands but with abruptness it can leave, giving a lift to the human spirit and planting a song in the hearts of children as the sun shines through to brighten the morning.

Summer is presented as a time of activity in which it seems that nature exists for human enjoyment. Boats can take you to out of the way places and bring you home again. A rock scarred by a glacier a million years ago provides children with a diving platform at high tide. At low tide the sand below becomes the setting for castles and roads.

Summer daytime guests leave behind them a sense of loneliness in the evening. However, the stars gaze down suggesting that "a hundred pairs of eyes are watching you," a thought which brings to the mind of the author that "one pair of eyes is watching over all." A reference to the Creator is appropriate in this natural setting of wonder and solitude.

In the Fall it is as if mother nature were growing old and a bit edgy. The boats are fewer and the winds more brisk. Some winds are so strong that boats don't venture out. On other days the harbors have about them the stillness of death. It's a time to be on the watch, to be prepared.

Eyeing the sky an old timer observes, "We're going to have some weather." Another native of the coast listens carefully to a loon and remarks, "It's a-comin'." The stillness in the air becomes heavy as nature joins in giving a warning all its own. The signs are there for those who have eyes to see and ears to hear.

It's a time for a quick trip to the mainland for food and gasoline. The chains that link cruise schooners to docks get checked, while the conversation in the store produces "ripples of its own." Talk is about hundred pound anchors, two inch ropes, and one inch chains. "Will they hold?"

The question both reflects and triggers apprehension, a concern for the unknown. The author notes how people hurry home to stock shelves with groceries and get ready for the worst. However, the rest of creation shares in the concern. One picture shows gulls sitting "solemnly" on a ledge, all looking in the same direction—toward the weather that's a-comin'. A mouse drags a stalk into its hole and a spider disappears into a crack in the bark of a tree.

The homes and the creatures that inhabit them are different, but at this time they share a common fear. No creature is too small or too large not to feel it and respond. There is a oneness here, the oneness of vulnerability.

The uninvited guest arrives, gently at first; the winds are mild. Suddenly, as if tired of introductions, it whips the water into waves. Rain pelts the earth and the wind snaps branches as if they were toothpicks protruding from a chunk of cheese. A gull, flying into the wind looking for a place to land, is actually being pushed backward. Trunks of trees also snap like toothpicks, and when they do you can't hear them because of the roar of the hurricane.

The unwelcome visitor blows open the door to a house strewing papers and a Parcheesi game across the floor. An illustration in the text shows a father leaning against the door. Finally he succeeds in pushing the windy visitor outside where it belongs.

The family attempts to drown out its fear by singing, or shouting "eyes have seen the glory." The "coming of the Lord" is left out as if the author is reluctant to make a direct link between nature's fury and the "pair of eyes that watch over all."

In the morning there are fallen trees everywhere, but with the havoc there are new wonders to behold. Parts of trees that were too far above to be climbed can now be walked upon safely by little children. They explore a gaping hole where the roots and base of a tree used to be. In it they find a pile of shells left there perhaps by Indian children centuries before. The hurricane reveals the shells for the first time.

Sunflowers flattened by the wind begin to slowly rise again. But the greatest wonder of all is that the hummingbirds circle the island one more time before heading south for the winter. It is a time of quiet questioning, the author suggests, wondering, for instance, "Where do hummingbirds go in a hurricane?" There is no answer, only the reminder of the "pair of eyes that watches over all." In the midst of the storm that seems to rage out of control there is a power of God at work revealing the capacity to care for this gentle, light and tiny creature, conveying the message "not to worry."

The illustrations in this book surround the words with feeling. We are really there during the storm rather than sitting safely in a classroom or snugly in a living room. We may call storms from the sea Gloria, Hazel, or Charles. We can name them but we cannot tame them, for they are not human after all. And that is part of the wonder.

Conversation Starters

- At what points in this story does the creation become one?

- What does the author mean by "one pair of eyes watching over all"?

- Where *do* hummingbirds go in a hurricane?

- Are the hummingbirds more in God's care than we are during one of nature's uproars?

Genetic Timekeeper

LEO, THE LATE BLOOMER
by Robert Kraus
32 pages
(New York: Windmill Books, 1971)

> *There appears to be some sort of inner clock at work in nature and in other parts of creation. Leo's growth is slower, but it happens. How this relates to God is one question this story brings to mind.*

Leo couldn't do anything right. He couldn't read. He couldn't write or draw. He couldn't eat without slopping food all over, and he couldn't talk. In a sense Leo wasn't even a lion. He was a tiger, a very young tiger.

As far as we know, no lion or tiger or any animal for that matter has ever talked, drawn, read, or written a line. The ascribing of human qualities to an animal is common in children's literature, nonetheless, just as ascribing human qualities to God is a common thing in other literature. Both are known by the same large word, anthropomorphism.

Late blooming is also a common experience for human beings. In this story Leo's father is the first to notice that Leo is late in accomplishing certain tasks. "What's the matter with Leo?" he asks one day. And with confidence and assurance the mother replies, "Nothing. Leo's just a later bloomer."

Present in the illustrations in this story is the reason the father asks the question. All the other tigers Leo's age are reading, writing, drawing, and talking. If they had all been like Leo then everything would have seemed normal and there would have been no questions. However, what this story underscores is that we are not all alike, even when it comes to growing up. "To everything there is a time and a season," goes the popular song, taking a cue from Ecclesiastes, Chapter Three. And at first one is tempted to place growing up under this directive.

However, in the story the mother's assurance is small consolation to the father. He watches for signs of Leo's coming of age day and night, but to no avail. He tries to watch TV to get his mind off Leo, but it isn't easy. Perhaps there is a shadow of doubt in his mind that Leo will bloom at all. That does happen to some members of a human family.

Finally the father gives up looking for Leo to bloom. Whether he gets tired of keeping watch or decides it is futile, we are not told. We are told that winter comes and Leo has not bloomed. Spring also comes and the flowers bloom but not Leo. Then the summer comes and suddenly Leo breaks out of himself. He can read, write, draw, and eat without messing up. And he can talk, not just one word but a sentence. He says, "I made it."

The theological issue for faith that this story perhaps unintentionally raises, but which is present, is: Why this difference between children? Is it because even to growing up there is a time, a season? Is it that the Creator has a predetermined schedule to follow, a timetable?

There does indeed seem to be a timetable when we take a look at what occurs in other realms of nature or creation. It is with awe and wonder that we watch the birds begin their southern flight in the fall, or read about salmon finding their way back to the very same stream in which they were born after spending their brief lifetime swimming in the ocean. Flowers, too, seem to be on some kind of "inner clock" when it comes to blooming and dying.

Jesus said that God even knows when a sparrow falls. But does that mean God decides in advance or on the spur of the moment when a bird is going to be born, or leave the nest, or die of old age? Is everything that lives and breathes controlled by God, every moment, every day, every hour? Is that what it means to say "In God we live and move and have our being"?

If so, what about those children who are non-bloomers? How about autistic children who never learn to talk, or those with dyslexia for whom reading is put off for many years or always done with difficulty? Can we talk about God's timetable and leave them out?

Or is God held back by some things? Are some things beyond God's control? The ministry of Jesus among us two centuries ago suggests that some of God's ideas and plans are met with resistance by people. People can throw up barriers and blockades in the pathway God might travel. What the story of Jesus also suggests is that God works with us, taking into account factors that we do not understand, but which obviously do not always work out right, at least not according to our plans and schedules.

There is a great deal of patience needed on both our part and God's when it comes to the human story. "Patience" may be a human term that does not apply to God; that is, God may not have to exercise "patience." However, we certainly do. It applies to us, and there are those who find their patience being renewed through faith in God.

This story touches a mystery that we have yet to plumb in relation to God, or one that God has not yet seen fit to reveal to us. However, it is a known reality, and talking about it with children can be of help not only to them but to parents as well. We do children in school an injustice when we expect all of them to progress at the same pace or hand out grades based on their failure to do so. It would be better if we at least left room for the mystery.

Conversation Starters

■ How do you think Leo felt about being a "late bloomer"?

■ How did his mother know that Leo was going to be one?

■ What part do you think God plays in this in real life?

■ What parts of the Bible speak to this meaningfully for you?

■ What parts raise questions?

ANNIE AND THE OLD ONE
by Miska Miles
44 pages
(Boston: Little, Brown, 1971)

> *A close relationship leads a Navajo granddaughter to try to prevent her grandmother's natural death, until the "Old One" says to the young one "You have tried to hold back time. It can't be done."*

With all the quiet determination of a general briefing his troops about the battle plan, a Navajo grandmother gathers her family around the small campfire one evening after supper and declares, "My children, when the new rug is taken from the loom, I will go to Mother Earth."

She isn't ailing that anyone can see, but she is old. Her face bears the leathery wrinkles of one who has spent years living in the outdoors.

I immediately thought of a handful of individuals I have known or heard about who arranged their affairs and then as if by some instinct died soon thereafter.

To Annie, the granddaughter, the announcement is a very unhappy thought. She loves her grandmother as much as her own mother. The bond between them is strong. They have gone for many walks together, and Annie just loves to listen to her tell stories about the past. These spontaneous interviews fill her spirit.

"How does she know?" Annie asks her mother shortly after the announcement.

"Many of the old ones know," the mother replies. "Your grandmother is one of those who live in harmony with all nature—with earth, coyote, birds in the sky. They know more than many will ever learn."

With that thought expressed by the author I expected a reference to the Great Spirit to appear, but the only reference to the Deity that surfaces in this story is a reference to the coyote as "God's Dog" guarding the hogans (shelters) of scattered Navajo families. Still there lingered in my mind the implicit meaning of being "in harmony with all nature." Whether mentioned or not it seemed to include the Creator of that harmony, and not just the dust that covers the top layers of Mother Earth.

Annie's response to this announcement is to wonder why her mother continues to weave on the loom. If completing the project means the death of her grandmother, then to her mind the reasonable thing to do is to not weave anymore. Stopping the weaver's stick seems the better part of her wisdom.

When her mother continues to weave in order to provide the family with income, Annie decides to take matters into her own hands. She purposely tries to get in trouble in school so her parents would have to come and talk to the teacher—leaving the loom untouched for a day. Unfortunately, it doesn't work. She doesn't get into trouble even when she hides a teacher's shoe.

When this fails she gets up very early in the morning and lets the sheep out of the fold, thinking they will get lost and require the time of both mother and father to find them, again another day away from the dreadful loom. That, too, fails. The sheep don't wander far enough away to get lost. And it is the grandmother who spots them and they are easily led back home.

Plan three is more serious. After everyone is asleep, she gets up in the middle of the night and goes to the loom where she pulls out strands of yarn one by one. She does this several nights and each morning her mother is puzzled that somehow the progress of the day before is reversed.

Her grandmother is not fooled, however. Quietly, tenderly, she takes Annie aside and says, "You have tried to hold back time. It can't be done." A profound thought—one that does not rest easily.

What might come to mind is the picture of miles of tubes that emerge from the nose and skin of elderly people in nursing homes and hospitals that keep them hooked up with "bottles of life" hanging from movable poles beside their beds. We have almost made an occupation out of holding back time. Nature has no chance to take its course the way it does with this grandmother from a Navajo Indian tribe.

And are persons who are kept alive by artificial means really alive? When, in fact, does a person die? When he or she stops breathing? Not necessarily. When the body is no longer capable of functioning or when the mind ceases to allow words to form on the lips, death has already made a down payment, or put in an appearance.

We may hold time back but we cannot stop it. "Time, like an ever rolling stream, soon bears us all away," as the hymn "O God Our Help In Ages Past" suggests.

The story of Annie and the Old One ends with Annie saying to her mother after more words from her grandmother, "I am ready to learn to weave now." She had declined this opportunity before, but now, sadder but infinitely wiser, she proceeds with life, knowing that it will bring her grandmother's announcement closer and closer to fulfillment with every strand of yarn that is added to the loom.

She learns a great lesson, one that some schools of modern medicine are slow to understand. God does have a timetable called nature, and if it is allowed to tick away, when we reach the sunset years, we will move more quickly to the Source of Life that beckons us all.

Conversation Starters

- Why does Annie ask her mother why she continues to weave?

- What prompts Annie to try to prolong her grandmother's life?

- In this story is there any hint of God's presence?

- In what way does modern medicine sometimes try to hold back time in the treatment of ailing elderly people? Does it succeed?

Death As Earth's Friend

TUCK EVERLASTING
by Natalie Babbitt
139 pages
(New York: Farrar, Straus, Giroux, 1975)

Winnie Foster discovers the Tuck family quite by accident. Though they are unusually kind people, their story is hard for her to believe. Still, she becomes involved in helping them keep their awesome secret because not to age is a heavy burden.

When Winnie Foster and Jesse Tuck meet each other in the Foster woods it leads to some strange conversations. Yet, when you stop to think about their words, they make sense.

To her innocent question "How old are you?" Jesse replies that he is one hundred and four, which causes Winnie to laugh. When she presses him for a serious response he replies "seventeen." Believe it or not, both answers are true.

Jesse is in the woods sitting by a tree next to a small fountain-like spurt of water rising up from some pebbles he has just removed. He is waiting for his mother whom he has not seen for ten years to meet him there.

The reader first knows something is odd about the Tucks when Mae, Jesse's mother, is getting dressed for the trip. The writer makes it clear that it is one of the hottest days in August. Yet Mae takes great pains to cover herself completely, even to the extent of wearing a shawl around her head so no one will see her. It is not necessary for her to see herself in the mirror because she already knows what she looks like. She has looked exactly the same for eighty-seven years—the difference between one hundred seven and twenty.

It was eighty-seven years before that the Tuck family rode through the woods. Spotting the small fountain of water they stopped for a drink, which in some ways was the worst thing they could have done. At first they didn't notice anything, though when Jesse fell out of a tree landing on his head it causes them to wonder why it didn't hurt him a bit. Then when some hunters mistake their horse for a deer and shoot it, the bullet goes clear through without even leaving a mark.

When they see that after ten years they have not changed at all, problems begin. Other folks notice too and the Tucks have to keep moving. Going through the same woods they come upon the stream again. They observe how the "T" Tuck had carved in the trunk of the tree is as fresh as if it had been cut yesterday and that the tree had not grown one inch. Then they realize it is the water. (Perhaps the water was left over from some plan for the way the world should be, a plan that didn't work out.) Their horse had drunk from the same stream.

They finally settle in a remote area, build a small house, and try to live. Jesse and his brother Miles go away for years at a time to work and earn some money for the family, careful to keep changing jobs so as not to arouse suspicion. Every ten years they come home. That's how Jesse met Winnie, waiting for his mother by the tree.

This part of the Tucks' story Winnie hears at their house, where they take her so they can figure out what to do. Mostly they want to make sure she won't tell anyone about the water. They want her to hear what agelessness is like. From their experience it does not fit in this world.

Winnie gets her first hint of this when Miles takes her fishing. Hearing him say that snapping turtles eat frogs, she naively observes, "It'd be nice if nothing ever had to die." Not only does Miles' picture of a world full of creatures "squeezed in right next to each other" cause her to think, but the thought of mosquitoes forever breeding and never dying makes her realize such a situation would be terrible.

She finds the Tucks very concerned about her welfare and how her parents must wonder where she is. However, it falls to Mr. Tuck to explain their situation in rather poignant terms so she hopefully will keep their secret. He notes how everything in this life is moving, growing, changing, except the Tucks. "We're stuck . . . left behind." He adds that "living's heavy work, and you can't have living without dying. So you can't call it living, what we got. We just *are*, we just *be*, like rocks beside the road."

The whole Tuck family loves Winnie, for she is the first person they have talked to outside their family for years. In fact, says Jesse, "You're the only person in the world, besides us, who knows about it." He refers to the water and what it does, but unbeknown to him that is not true. Miles had married at one point but separated when his wife kept getting older while he stayed the same age. The weird tales this spawned found their way to the ears of a man who sees the water as a way of making a lot of money.

The day Winnie is brought to the Tucks' house, this man, who has been searching for "the family," follows her and overhears the first part of their story. He then returns to the Fosters who are indeed beside themselves with worry over their Winnie's disappearance. He offers to make a trade: the deed to the woods for information on where their daughter is. "I've got what you want and you've got what I want." They do not know the water is there but he knows and he doesn't tell them.

They really have no idea what he wants, but when he shows up at the Tucks' with the town constable it doesn't take the Tucks long to discover what he wants and why. The story moves to a dramatic conclusion when Mae Tuck hits him over the head with an old rifle and he dies. The constable arrests her, and when it appears that she may be the first person to hang on the town's brand new gallows, the last and most terrible problem with agelessness on Earth is raised. She would hang there and not die. What is done to help her out of this dilemma I will leave for the reader to find out. The story is beautifully told and is hard to put down once one begins to read it. There are a number of turns and twists including the finale which I have left out of this synopsis.

The point of the tale seems to be that as pleasant sounding as life everlasting may sound in the face of death, on Earth or in this life it is out of place. It is not compatible with life as we know it, and in a most unusual manner the reader gains what amounts to an appreciation for this life and the part death plays in it. There is far more to this story than a modern day tale about a fountain of youth.

Of course, the story is implausible. The little spring of water may remind a reader of what Jesus referred to as "living water," but curiously enough, not even that reference fits in this life when one pursues the implications in the way Natalie Babbitt has. Such water is reserved for life after we have made our exit from this one through the doorway called death.

Conversation Starters

- Why do you think the Tucks are such kind and gentle people?

- How would you answer the question about the ownership of land the story raises?

- How do you feel about Jesse's proposal to Winnie that she drink some of the water when she reaches his age—seventeen—and then they would get married?

- How did you feel about the ending in the Tucks' return to the town years later, after Winnie had grown old and died?

What Makes a Garden Grow?

FROG AND TOAD TOGETHER
by Arnold Lobel
64 pages
(New York: Harper & Row, 1972)

> *In this ongoing saga of Frog and Toad, we see Toad's inclination to interpret Frog's words about planting a garden in ways Frog never dreams of. Frog's patience is of an infinite quality.*

For most of us, "frogs" and "toads" are two names for the same hind leg leaping creatures. Although biologically one is more land oriented than the other, in these stories there is another difference, namely, intelligence. Frog is the leader of the two, and Toad the follower, as in the picture of the two on the cover pedaling a two-seated bicycle. In this series of short stories Frog is repeatedly cast in the role of helping Toad do simple things, such as planting a garden.

Frog has a garden, and because of that Toad would like one also. His slowness of wit contributes to some humorous moments, but never does Frog laugh at him, ridicule him, or criticize him. In this book of five stories, the story titled "The Garden" is a good example. Frog seems blessed with seemingly endless patience.

Frog notes in the beginning that having a garden is hard work and this is the first of two misunderstandings that set the framework for the story. The other is immediately after Frog gives Toad some seeds and tells him to plant them. Toad's only concern is how soon he will have a garden like Frog's. "Quite soon," replies Frog and it becomes clear that his understanding of "soon" and that of Toad's are rather different.

The plot thickens when Toad plants the seeds only to see that they do not produce instant plants. He assumes that talking to them will help, but when they do not answer he bends closer to the ground and talks more loudly, as if they are hard of hearing. When he then begins to shout at them, it brings Frog over on the run wondering what all the noise is about.

Tactfully, gracefully, Frog suggests in terms that his friend might understand that Toad's shouting is scaring the seeds. "These poor seeds are afraid to grow." Frog also recommends leaving them alone for a few days to let the sun shine on them, and the rain to water them.

Toad's eagerness to have a garden like Frog's makes it hard for him to hear his friend's advice. That very night he looks out his window to see if the seeds are growing, and when he does not see this, he concludes they are afraid of the dark. Thus, he sets up some candles in the ground above the seeds, and just to add a measure of security, he reads them a story. Little children might find this most amusing since they know all too well that seeds cannot hear, are not human, and that Toad's effort is not necessary even though it is nighttime—a time when children are sometimes afraid.

The next day Toad adds singing to his seed program, then poetry reading, and finally violin playing. Those who believe that plants respond to kind words have nothing on Toad.

When all his efforts seem in vain, Toad decides his seeds are the most frightened seeds in the world, and having done all he can think of he feels very tired. Soon he is fast asleep.

He awakens to the words of his friend Frog telling him that his seeds are growing. And as if he never heard Frog's words about the need for sunshine, rain and time, Toad agrees that now he, too, has a garden, but "it was very hard work."

The story ends there, but as we know, for Toad the hard work to which Frog also had referred is only beginning. Actually, the only thing Toad has contributed to the garden up to now is to put the seeds into the ground. However, from now on he will indeed have to work hard to keep the weeds from taking over.

This story, with Toad's inability to comprehend what makes seeds grow, has both first century and twentieth century overtones.

In the first century, Paul admitted that human beings may help "seeds" by "watering" them, but "only God gives the increase" or causes them to grow. The seeds to which Paul refers in First Corinthians, Chapter Three, verses 6 and 7, are those of faith, and it is partly in that connection that this story takes on meaning. The author does not speak of either faith or God but the story has a parable-like quality.

Just as Toad shouted in vain at the seeds to make them grow, so does his misunderstanding of how things grow shout at us. Whether it is raising children or flowers there is very little parents can do to make children grow physically any faster than the genetic timetable allows. There is even some doubt as to how much parents can do to enable children to grow emotionally or spiritually, except perhaps provide a warm, loving climate in which the "seeds" can grow. Even then children from the same family can turn out quite differently, as many parents know.

The other point at which this story takes a theological twist is in the relation of Frog and Toad. The boundless nature of Frog's patience illustrates something of the Creator's patience toward us. For a Frog, to say nothing of a human being, to be endowed with such a quality lifts the story to a theological level because only God possesses such infinite qualities.

Conversation Starters

■ What is the glue that holds Frog and Toad's friendship together?

■ What things that Frog says does Toad not hear?

■ Are there any ways that we are like either Frog or Toad?

■ How is Frog like God?

Nature's Uncanny Creatures

THE CRY OF THE CROW
by Jean Craighead George
149 pages
(New York: Harper & Row, 1980)

A pet crow walks and talks its way into the heart of a girl. When young, the crow thinks it is a person. When older, the crow's memory of who killed her parents leads the girl into making a difficult decision for the sake of her brother.

"Strictly for the birds" is a demeaning phrase, one that perhaps most people including Fred Tressel and his sons would apply to crows. However, his daughter Mandy experiences a keen admiration for crows, especially one whom she names Nina Terrance, "the name she would have given herself if she had had a choice."

Mandy awakens one morning to a shotgun blast and later that day finds the lone surviving member of a crow family huddled in fear underneath a tree in a nearby wooded area of the Florida everglades. Unable to feed itself, Mandy becomes the crow's substitute mother. She nourishes this dependency at first for the bird's own protection and later for Mandy's own needs.

She discovers that crows have two languages—their own and words they learn from people. The first people words Nina Terrance utters are "I got you"—the words spoken by the hunter who killed her parents. Crows tend to remember words they hear when they are severely frightened and can even remember the person who spoke them. Since they can distinguish one person from another, this trait is both a blessing and a curse in the story.

By observing sounds and effects Mandy learns the crow language. Highly organized and social birds, they take turns serving as guard crows always on the alert for hunters and other dangers. "Ca! Ca! Ca!

Ca!" is an alarm signal and Mandy learns to mimic it so she can protect her young pet. When she does, the bird cowers in fright and remains "stone still." Even the sight of a gun triggers the Ca cry from the guard crow. When the danger passes, the guard sounds the "all clear" cry, and the crows in the area relax and go about their bird routines.

One of the funniest parts in the story is when Nina Terrance distracts a mean dog so Mandy can walk by her house in safety. Flying near the dog's nose, the crow teases it and then leads it on an exhausting chase away from Mandy. This form of protection given by the crow reflects a personal experience in the life of the author, Jean George. I heard her tell how she, too, had several pet crows (as revealed on the dedication page of this book) and one would accompany her children to the school bus each morning. Upon seeing them safely on board, the crow would fly home and enter the house through a kitchen window left open for that purpose. Other children on the street were escorted to the bus by a parent. Jean George's children were escorted by a crow.

Mandy's father and older brothers shoot crows to protect their strawberry crop which is the family livelihood. Mr. Tressel becomes such an authority on strawberries that Cornell College invites him to Ithaca, New York, to share his wisdom. He takes the boys with him, and no sooner have the men left than Mandy hears a tap at the front door. Nina Terrance is standing there with other crows perched in a nearby tree crying out in alarm. As long as the men are home no crows come into the yard. The birds know who the hunters are and where they live. But now while the men are gone, Nina Terrance and even Old Kray walk and hop into the house and Nina makes herself quite at home, even to the point of opening the refrigerator door with her beak and helping herself to food.

One day Mandy, while pushing her way through a crowd at the town's shopping mall, is surprised to find Nina Terrance the center of attention. She has a box top in her beak and uses it to slide down a board, much to the amusement of the crowd gathered around her. What makes it even more eventful is that the TV Eyewitness News is also present filming the crow, the crowd, and also Mandy when she tells them the bird talks. Fortunately Nina Terrance demonstrates her ability to talk in a very entertaining way.

The most surprising thing about the newscast is that Mandy's father and brothers see it on TV while they are away. Mr. Tressel calls home and to Mandy's pleasant surprise states that she can keep the crow. Mandy had not told him about her new pet for fear her father would want to get rid of the potential thief of strawberries.

Permission to keep the crow comes at a time when Nina Terrance is being coaxed by the older crows to leave Mandy and fly away. Their cries touch off "ancient emotions," one of which is that when young crows grow up they disperse to other regions. Intuitively they do this to prevent the dangers of interbreeding, and to preserve the gene pool. Mandy hears her mother say that she too will do this some day. Birds and humans leave the nest.

Unfortunately, the aging process touches off another ancient emotion in Nina Terrance. "How vindictive are crows?" Mandy asks her mother one day. It is a crucial question because she has learned that it was her younger brother who shot and killed Nina's parents, and Nina has taken to harassing him. His fear for his life causes Mandy to make a difficult decision, one I will let readers find out for themselves because it makes for a poignant, maturing conclusion to this fascinating story.

Jean George at no point speaks of God in this story or even hints at the Creator's connection. However, the book is filled with awesome things that crows do, thus begging the question, "How can this be?" Many other animals have remarkable abilities such as whales who can hear sounds miles away and sharks who have a powerful sense of smell, so crows are by no means the only members of the animal world that possess exceptional qualities. That God created these animals this way is not mentioned but this thought certainly can occur to anyone familiar with the story of creation.

Conversation Starters

■ Why does Mandy like crows?

■ Would she have liked them if they ate many of her family's strawberries?

■ What makes *The Cry of the Crow* believable?

■ All puns aside, would you say this is a story to crow about? Why or why not?

Law and Gospel in a Classroom

MISS NELSON IS MISSING
by Harry Allard
30 pages
(Boston: Houghton Mifflin, 1977)

This story is a two day episode from an elementary school class-room. However, inside and underneath this educational situation there is a classical theological parable, one everyone can understand.

Room 207 looks like an elementary school version of a Blackboard Jungle. Spit balls are stuck to the ceiling. Paper airplanes sail through the air. Chaos reigns supreme. When a sweet voiced teacher says, "Now settle down," it is to no avail. Her words fall on deaf ears.

One might surmise that this sweet voice belongs to a harassed sub-stitute whom young students are taking complete charge of, but not so. This is the voice of the regular teacher, which the jacket of this book describes as the nicest teacher in the school. She never yells, always smiles, and gives easy assignments. However, that last characteristic carries with it a dubious distinction.

The children giggle, make faces and refuse to do their lessons. They are even unruly during story hour. The scene has something of a caricature to it. It is hard to imagine either a teacher or students be-having this way in response to each other. However, there is more to this story than meets the eye and ear. It contains surprises and deep meaning.

The first surprise is that Miss Nelson, the gentle, soft-spoken teacher, decides to do something. The reader discovers a teacher who really wants to have a pleasant working relationship with her students, one who believes that teaching and learning are not only easier but more effective that way. The point of the story is how she creates that relationship.

29

The next morning Miss Nelson does not show up for her class. Instead, a woman with a long nose and a pointed chin appears, like that of the witch in the story of Hansel and Gretel. She is wearing a black dress and her name is Miss Swamp.

"Open those arithmetic books," she barks, and suddenly, abruptly, the children do just that as if a jolt of lightning had touched their brain cells. In a tone of voice that frightens and words that intimidate she commands them to "keep their mouths shut" and "sit still." She not only announces there will be no story hour that day, she also lays homework on them, the likes of which they had never seen with Miss Nelson.

What the reader is confronting at this moment in the story the book jacket succinctly sums up in the words "Miss Swamp immediately lays down the law." In appearance and tone of voice she is the law, for the law's effect is not exactly a boost to the human spirit. As Paul writes in Romans 13, the law is a terror to bad conduct.

While extra-curricular activity is par for the course, some of the children in Room 207 embark on a unique quest; they begin to hunt for Miss Nelson. They speculate on what might have happened to her and finally decide to go to her house. This approach is quickly aborted, however, when they spot Miss Swamp, of all persons, coming around the corner of Miss Nelson's house. At the sight of her they do a quick about face and run for their lives.

The children begin to think that Miss Nelson will never come back and the thought of having Miss Swamp there permanently is very discouraging. Just when they are the most depressed they hear footsteps in the hall and a sweet voice says, "Hello, children."

"Where were you?" they ask, and she replies, "That's my little secret." During the story hour when the children pay close attention and the rudeness and silliness seem to have disappeared, she inquires slyly, "What brought about this lovely change?"

"That's our little secret," the children respond.

When she returns to her home at the end of the school day, Miss Nelson hangs her coat in the closet next to an ugly black dress. At this point parents and teachers can have great fun with children in asking if they know Miss Nelson's secret.

Near the end of the story Miss Nelson is saying to herself, "I'll never tell," and the reader can get the feeling that perhaps she is saving her change of costume and personality for a new class next year. The author has written other books about Miss Nelson and her class, one of which is *Miss Nelson Returns* in which a similar process is repeated.

Miss Nelson succeeded in creating a climate for teaching the way she feels is best for learning, but there is much more going on here than an illustration of a teacher changing the climate in her classroom.

This story in a most intriguing manner both in words and in pictures is in touch, perhaps unwittingly, with a universal experience of human nature and how to deal with it redemptively. Miss Swamp and Miss Nelson represent what some theologians refer to as law and gospel, a dualism that runs deep in the Old and New Testaments and everyone's personal history.

In Miss Swamp we have a portrayal of the demands and threats that are present in parts of the Bible. They are present even in the confrontation Jesus had with the scribes and Pharisees in the temple where he spoke of them as hypocrites and pronounced woe to them because of what they were doing to people. It is the same tone of law being laid down, judgment being administered.

In the thinking of Paul in the New Testament (Galatians 3:24) the law is present as a "schoolmaster" for the purpose of cultivating the climate for the good news of the gospel, for grace. Miss Nelson is the epitome of grace in the classroom, but before the children can appreciate it they have to have an experience with the law, with what some might call "wrath."

The contrast between law and gospel creates appreciation for the gospel. The law threatens; the gospel comforts. The law commands; the gospel offers love and forgiveness. The law produces despair (discouragement in the children's case); the gospel gives peace and hope. The changed atmosphere in the classroom is a testament to this dynamic at work.

The law is apropos when we are not receptive to the gospel. Miss Swamp is necessary when we are not able or willing to respond to Miss Nelson. Miss Nelson has the capacity to lay down the law, to come down hard on children. However, she does not like herself this way and does not genuinely believe that learning takes place in a climate of intimidation. It may be necessary at some times in order to get respect for learning, but when it has been established it is the good relationship between teachers and children, or parents and children, that allows understanding to take place.

Conversation Starters

- Why did Miss Nelson show up one day as Miss Swamp?

- Are there teachers and parents who combine both law (sternness) and gospel (kindness) and use them at different times?

- Why is it at times necessary to "lay down the law"?

- Why is it hard for learning to occur in an atmosphere of fear?

- What does this story tell us about God's relationship to us and vice versa?

Unemployment

RAMONA AND HER FATHER
by Beverly Cleary
186 pages
(New York: Dial Press, 1977)

Forced into an unemployment situation a father comes to ap-
preciate his daughter. She helps him. The story reinforces why
Jesus placed such importance on small children.

Ramona and her sister knew something was wrong when their parents talked in whispers. What they were concerned about was that their
father had lost his job. For young families who are experiencing a similar situation this story provides numerous points of identification, hu-
mor, and hope.

Ramona's first response is to think of ways to help the family income, and her mind begins generating ideas when she hears that the
young boy on TV doing an ad probably gets a million dollars for it. She
can think of a lot of things she could do with that much money, beginning with turning up the thermostat so they would not have to wear
sweaters in the house to save fuel oil. She learns, however, that what
is repeated often in a TV ad does not have the same effect in real life.

One point of identification is that a small child can provide a dis-
traction from the bread and butter worries that come with a job loss.
(The mother works outside the home but one income is not the same
as two.) For example, while the father is talking with her teacher during
a parent-teacher conference, Ramona finds some burrs that stick together well. When she makes a crown out of them and plunks them
down on her head, it is her father who patiently works to remove them
one at a time.

On another occasion the father tackles the job of making a face on
the Halloween pumpkin someone has given him. This not only delights

the family, but gives him a boost because he is the best pumpkin carver on the block. Unusual patience emerges when the cat—tired of cheaper food—begins eating the pumpkin during the night, and another face on another pumpkin has to be carved.

Nevertheless, unemployment is not easy to live with. It takes a toll on the father and the family even in this story. Nerves become frayed. The father's personality seems to change. Each time the phone rings there is the hope that a job offer is at the other end.

One important point in this book is that small children do worry about parents. In this family the news that smoking can cause cancer prompts the daughters to initiate a no smoking crusade to get the father to stop. They try many things, such as "no smoking" signs on the walls, and rolling up pieces of paper and replacing the cigarettes in a pack with the newly made fake ones. The father sees this as an indication of their care for him and eventually promises to try to stop.

A touching moment occurs when Ramona smells smoke in the living room and the father acknowledges how hard it is to quit. It is as if her father in being honest with her was treating her as an adult confidante. This means a lot to Ramona. Their relationship is special.

This special relationship is highlighted in other ways in the story. Her father uses his time wisely at home doing things with her, such as making the longest sign in the world. He also sometimes escapes by watching TV.

Although Ramona prays that her father will get another job, which he does near the end of the story, that does not prevent her panic and guilt feelings one afternoon when she comes home from school and he is not there. The house is locked, and as she sits on the front steps in the rain she begins to imagine he has left because of her no smoking campaign. When he returns later and explains how the unemployment check line was long, she quickly relates to "long lines" from experiences in school, and feels relieved.

Ramona may be too young to fully appreciate the significance of unemployment, but she knows it will affect her Christmas list—things she wants to receive—and the family's going out for whopperburgers on pay day. However, two biblical overtones that one can pick up while reading this story are that families do bear one another's burdens, and that a "little child shall lead them."

Exasperating as small children can be sometimes, at other times they are teachers, not just pupils. It brings to mind the importance Jesus attached to children when he made one of them the model of his kingdom and placing the child in the midst of his adult followers he observed how no one is greater.

While it is not noted in this story, it is necessary to acknowledge that not all individuals or families survive unemployment. Not all have supporting families and there can be a split over such concerns. Some child abuse might be due to the frustration that can happen with the loss of a job over a long period of time. This story is realistic, but whether it would be sufficient to bind up some of the wounds may depend on how early in the experience it is read. One thing is certain. It would be therapeutic for a father and daughter to read together, and if the father is the one out of work they would have the time.

Conversation Starters

- How would you describe the relationship between Ramona and her father?

- In what ways is their relationship true-to-life?

- In what ways might it be unusual?

- What does Ramona learn about TV ads that have children in them that she did not know before?

- What does Ramona see in the wink her father gives her during the church Christmas program?

- In what way might God be at work in this family and in their situation?

A Little Acceptance Goes a Long Way

ALEXANDER AND THE TERRIBLE, HORRIBLE, NO GOOD, VERY BAD DAY
by Judith Viorst
30 pages
(New York: Atheneum, 1972)

> *It wasn't just a bad day; nothing at all went right. From waking up in the morning with gum in his hair to having lima beans for supper Alexander was miserable. Why?*

Days when nothing seems to go right do happen. For some, the situation can stretch to even longer periods of time. Many assume that this may be limited, however, to adults. This story suggests that it can also be the experience of young children.

The key issue is "Why?" Why was this such a bad day? The issue is raised on the book jacket, but the answer is left up to the reader.

The most immediate response to reading the story is to conclude that Alexander brought this day upon himself. After all, it was Alexander who went to sleep with gum in his mouth. If he wakes up to find it in his hair he has no one else to blame but himself. Preoccupied with this he trips over the skateboard which he had left on the floor from the night before.

There is clearly an emphasis in the story on "Alexander's state of mind" and it shows up very early in the morning. On the way down to breakfast, in fact, he has already decided that it is going to be a terrible, horrible, no good, very bad day. It is easy to assume at this point that there is a need for the power of positive thinking.

Indeed, there almost seems to be a measure of self-fulfilling prophecy at work in the story. With his mind made up, the day turns out just as he thinks it will. Even wars can begin this way. We think someone is an enemy and after we have built up our defenses we are convinced of it, and sure enough one day it occurs—a war breaks out.

With Alexander, however, there is another factor to be taken into consideration—that of not being responded to or even noticed. For example, on the way to school when Alexander finds himself scrunched between two friends in the back seat and he tells the others in the car about it, "No one even answered."

Those very same words slip from his lips when school is over. His foot gets stuck in the elevator door and while he is in pain standing on one leg holding his foot a brother bumps into him knocking him into a puddle of mud. When this produces some tears both brothers call him a crybaby. And when this causes him to explode in anger toward his brothers, his mother shows up in the car and scolds him for fighting with his brothers. At this point the young man says "I am having a terrible, horrible, no good, very bad day" to everybody, but again "No one even answered."

It would seem that he might be due a measure of sympathy. After all, at school that day his best friend's picture of a sailboat was liked more by the teacher than Alexander's picture of an "invisible castle." It is not known whether this means he handed in a blank page, but he seems to feel, nonetheless, that she should not have reacted that way and when he transfers some of these feelings to his friends, he drops a notch or two on their list.

It is important to note that not everything is his fault. His mother does forget to put some dessert in his lunch pail, and in a shoestore his brothers get sneakers with stripes on them, but he has to settle for white ones which he hates; there are no more striped sneakers left.

In any event it is amazing that no one shows him an ounce of sympathy. One cannot help but wonder if that might not be one reason the day was such a bad one. When no one else seems to care you have to provide sympathy for yourself which too easily turns into self-pity, a poison that doesn't help at all.

Filled with such feelings the only thing Alexander sees at the supper table are the lima beans. When watching TV the only thing he sees is the kissing. There is obviously more to supper than lima beans and more on TV than kissing, but his vision is now so filled with his own misery, it is all he can see.

The only solution the little lad sees to his misfortune is to move to Australia. However, in one simple line his mother provides what he has needed all day—sympathy, empathy, or understanding. Some might call it grace. She says, "Some days are like that . . . even in Australia." In these few words the author portrays the mother accepting Alexander and all the feelings and the reasons for them. Implicit in her words is her own personal experience of such days and the implication that there are apt to be bad days everywhere, and that maybe tomorrow will be better.

It is amazing what a night's rest can do, providing one removes the gum from his or her mouth before going to sleep. Things can look pretty grim at the end of the day, but somehow seem better in the morning. There was a rule in the household of Rose Kennedy never to share bad news at night if it was received then, but to wait until the next day when members of the family would be refreshed and more able to bear it.

It is as if while we sleep the God who never sleeps is at work cleaning our inner gears, giving us a fresh start. This common experience has led someone to assert that each new day is a day of grace.

In keeping with the author's desire that we ask "why" Alexander had such a bad day, some of the following questions might be used in the search for the reason or reasons with small children.

Conversation Starters

■ What started things off wrong for Alexander?

■ What does it mean when we say someone "got up on the wrong side of the bed"?

■ What things were clearly his fault?

■ What things were not his fault?

■ How does it feel to be blamed for something that was not your fault?

■ Why was it that no one sympathized with him during the day?

■ What effect could his mother's words have had on him if he had heard them earlier in the day?

Understanding God in Daily Life

ARE YOU THERE, GOD? IT'S ME, MARGARET
By Judy Blume
149 pages
(Englewood Cliffs: Bradbury, 1970)

A nearly twelve year old girl is the product of a mixed marriage. Though she has "no religion," she is very religious. She shares with God what others might write in a diary. She interprets experiences as God's way of responding to her.

It may seem like a long jump from *Playboy*'s centerfold to a twelve year old girl's prayer content, but Judy Blume makes it seem like a very natural, short step. In fact, in this story the two are intimately joined.

At almost twelve a young girl is changing physically but not according to her expectations, and the part of the anatomy that receives its fantasy laden proportions from the above magazine causes all sorts of anxiety for Margaret Simon.

Along with a missing measurement in her anatomy, Margaret is made to feel that something else is missing in her life. As one of her friends put it when introducing Margaret to her minister, "She's no religion."

A combination of sex and religion are the motifs of this story, and for some readers this may be the reason the book is on their controversial list. They see sex as "dirty" and religion as "clean" and never the twain should meet.

The gap between "religion" and "reality" which this view creates is filled in by Judy Blume in a way that reveals numerous insights into the way God works in human life and the way the church relates or does not relate to "outsiders"—those who are presently the majority in the United States.

The clue that there is something sincere and deep going on in

Margaret's relation to God emerges when her girl friends say she is lucky she doesn't have to go to Sunday School. One might think this "witness" would undercut her desire to visit churches and a Jewish temple, but no, it doesn't undermine this desire at all.

Margaret's state of having "no religion" results from her father being Jewish and her mother coming from a Christian background. Margaret's parents have decided to let Margaret decide for herself what religion she wants to follow when she chooses to do so.

Margaret receives two views or influences from her grandparents, who from their Jewish and Gentile backgrounds each urge her to go their way. Caught in the middle, Margaret determines to settle it for herself. In that way she can go to either the YWCA or the Jewish Community Center. One of Margaret's ways of trying to settle it is to make a study of religion a term paper topic in school.

She promises to make no decision without checking with God first, and this introduces a very contemporary phenomenon in American life, the separation in many minds between God and the church.

The necessity for "religion" is implicit in this story, but not before the reader is clearly exposed to a young girl who is already very religious, or should we say "devotional," in her relation to the Deity.

The author includes in italics Margaret's "talk" to God at the end of a chapter or sometimes in the midst of one, the way a person might add lines to a diary at the end of a day. However, in this case the diary is like talking to God—the recipient of each day's "entry."

The first half of the book's title, *Are You There, God?* is at the beginning of each "conversation" even when at a low point in her life she remembered "I wasn't talking to him anymore."

This salutation is appropriate for a couple of reasons. It first and foremost fits the universal situation between God and us, that God is unseen and never answers us in audible words the way we express our thoughts to God in words, audibly or silently. *Are You There, God? It's Me, Margaret* is like seeking the attention of a friendly ghost that one believes is in the room but cannot see.

It also expresses what a thoughtful person or a skeptic may feel—that God is not accessible with direct immediacy. This is also the experience of some church attenders, but they might not admit it except in more candid moments because much that is heard in church conveys the impression that God is always there waiting to be the other partner in a two-way communication.

Most of the story proceeds without reference to Margaret's one-way "conversations" with God. In fact, the two-way conversations that are recorded are between Margaret and her girl friends and with boys at school and at parties.

Woven into these conversations, however, is the anxiety and cause for Margaret's calling upon the Deity. Fear is a primary motive—fear of moving into a new neighborhood, fear of not developing as a young girl in the right places, fear of what happens to her father when he mows the lawn, fear of not getting a good grade in a test, and fear of not getting to dance with a certain boy at a party. Nevertheless, these prayer requests always end with "Thank you." It is as if God is present while she is in the process of expressing herself.

Her "religion" project reveals a profound but unsettling bit of reality. She goes to church expecting to find God there, but never does in the way she does at home during her private prayers. The sermon and prayers in church are beyond her understanding; they convey the strong message that the language employed is for "insiders only."

Even when she attends a Christmas Eve service she enjoys the music very much but, as she states in one of her prayers, "Still, I didn't really feel you, God." This confuses her, for somehow, despite being of "no religion," she has the image of God being in church in a special way. Consequently, she completes her term paper on religion not knowing what religion to become, but convinced that one has to be introduced to it much earlier in life in order to understand it. There is something intriguing in the fact that she says several times that God doesn't seem too eager to help her decide which religion to be.

A low point in her life occurs when she has paid too much attention to what her friends are saying about another girl in her class named Laura. Acting on this gossip she hurts Laura's feelings very much and subsequently Margaret feels that God is punishing her for this by not letting her go to visit her Jewish grandmother in Florida whom she loves dearly. To God she says, "I'm definitely the most horrible person who ever lived and I really don't deserve anything good to happen to me." That this act of contrition occurs without her having a contact with the church is a thought-provoking point in this book.

Even when Margaret feels alienated from God she is close to God. She expresses anger with God at one point, and dares God to punish her when she crosses the street against the light but "Nothing happened!" This is her first clue that perhaps God is not punishing her, and does not work that way as she had assumed.

Of great concern to Margaret is not having had her first period, and she feels God is punishing her in this way also. It has somehow become a "rite of passage" among her friends. However, when at this low point, and feeling horrible because of what she said to Laura, she gets her first period, it is something for which she is most grateful to God. The story ends on this note with Margaret's final "entry":

> Are you still there, God? It's me, Margaret. I know you're there, God. I know you wouldn't have missed this for anything! Thank you, God. Thanks an awful lot. . . .

The one thing that "church" could add to her life is an understanding of what she is experiencing in relation to God. Speaking as one who has participated in the life of the church my entire life, what Margaret experiences at the end could be interpreted as unmerited grace. She feels "horrible" as a person. She feels that perhaps she has offended God. But given the importance she and her friends attach to the commencement of the menstrual cycle, it becomes for her an indication that God is responding to her request. Grace would be meaningful at this point, but she would perhaps have to be in church or have somone interpret it in such terms for it to be understood.

Conversation Starters

■ Why does God seem further from Margaret in church than at home?

■ When we stop to think about it, how much does fear enter into our "prayers"?

■ Is there any truth to the idea that much of the language in church or synagogue is for "insiders"? If so, why is this?

- Does God punish us for hurting the feelings of someone, or for doing something harmful to them?

- Where might Margaret have gotten the idea that God is punishing her?

- Why is there a gap in church between religion and real life? How does God fit into this gap?

A Wisdom Greater Than Ours

THE WISH GIVER
by Bill Brittain
181 pages
(New York: Harper & Row, 1983)

> *When a stranger sells each of three children a ticket that will provide them with one thing they want most, he warns them to be very careful what they choose. Unfortunately, they do not heed his advice soon enough.*

Many states in our country are introducing a lottery as a way of raising money. People buy tickets and indicate what they hope will be the lucky number. When no one wins the purse grows, and when it is large the lines waiting to buy tickets can get very long. All of these people would just love to win. All of them probably have some idea as to what they would do with the money if they did. However, the odds of their winning are slim. There is hardly any hope, and certainly no assurance connected with it.

For three teenagers, Polly, Rowena, and Adam, who attend the Coven Tree Church Social, the odds are quite different. They are assured by one Thaddeus Blinn, a little man lurking on the edge of the crowd, that for fifty cents he will give each of them a ticket good for one wish, and that whatever they wish for will come true. He says there are no limits. "Anything you could possibly imagine can be yours." He does warn them—twice—that they must think very carefully about what they want, since their wish will come true.

At first the youngsters are incredulous. They each buy one ticket with a red spot on it, but each puts it away thinking it is a hoax. However, one by one each reaches a dire point in his or her life and turns to the ticket, rubs the spot, and the wish does indeed come true, though not quite as they expect.

Polly's wish seems the most harmless of all. After being humiliated by a rich girl outside of church one Sunday, a girl she greatly admires, she wishes that people will pay attention to her, smile when they see her, and that the rich girl will invite her to her house someday soon.

Her wish begins coming true very quickly, the very next morning to be exact. Experiencing irritation, she bluntly tells her mother the toast "is just horrid. It's all burned and—JUG-A-RUM!" Her next word, in the middle of the sentence, is the exact sound of a bull frog. And for a while, that is the only word she can speak. She has a tendency for telling people precisely what she thinks, and it has not won her many friends. Her need for attention and to be liked is strong.

For the next couple of days whenever Polly dishes out one of her blunt retorts, she croaks like a frog. As one can imagine it gets her much attention and no end of smiles. It even gets her an invitation to the rich girl's house who wants to trick her into anger so she will croak like a frog in front of her mother.

What takes place, however, is that Polly realizes what is happening and is highly motivated to not display her true feelings anymore when someone or something gets her angry. She discovers that by curbing her tongue she begins to win attention and smiles, genuine smiles, without croaking. She even discovers at the rich girl's house that Agatha is so restricted by her wealth she is missing much in life.

Rowena's wish is that a young, good-looking traveling salesperson, Henry Piper, will put down roots in Coven Tree and never leave. No sooner wished than done, unfortunately. Henry is walking away from Rowena's house when his feet seem to stick to the ground. He can't move another step. When Rowena and another young man who works for her father come to help, they discover that roots are growing up through Henry's shoes from the ground. By the next day he has become a tree firmly planted in the grove on the property owned by Rowena's father. As the transformation takes place Henry, understandably upset, reveals that he does not care for Rowena at all and is just using his friendship with her to sell her father farm machinery. She feels badly, first for what happens to Henry but then for what she finds out about him.

Adam's wish is that there might be water all over his parent's farm. "Enough for washing and cooking and drinking and for the crops, and . . . with plenty to spare, too!" His wish is logical. There is no water on the piece of land his father farms and consequently it falls to Adam to go down to the creek on the other side of town with three tubs, fill them, and cart them through town back home whenever there is a period of no rain. He, too, finds this embarrassing. Kids make fun of him. "I guess they're getting mighty thirsty out there" someone inevitably says.

As you can imagine, after the wish there is plenty of water. It comes up everywhere. In fact it keeps on spouting and soon the house, which is in a lower part of the property, is surrounded by water. It looks like a boat on a lake. His family has to leave but they end up on new property that at least has water.

What each youngster fails to consider is that the Wish Giver takes them literally. Each is moved by self-interest, but also learns something in the process. If they did not think at first, the results of their wishes cause them to think a great deal about what they have done, what they want, and what matters most in life.

One natural question this raises is who is Thaddeus Blinn. A storekeeper who helps cancel the effect of their wishes with his own ticket saw a look in Blinn's eyes which he links with the devil. But one must remember that Thaddeus urges the children not once but twice to think carefully about what they will wish for. Moreover, in each case something good comes out of the disastrous effect of their wishing. Each wish becomes a blessing in disguise.

The reader perhaps has two ways of viewing this situation, or of interpreting it, both related to God. One is called "monism" and the other "dualism." Monism is a word for "one" and would suggest that God is at work in Thaddeus Blinn from the beginning. Dualism is a word for "two" and means here that the devil is working in the guise of Blinn, but God is at work to outwit him, to bring good out of evil . . . and succeeds.

There are, to be sure, many things in creation that seem perfectly harmless to wish for, things that would be helpful, things that are products of creation, or God's handiwork. We simply have to learn how to use them with care. This reinforces the monism interpretation. On the other hand, what we know of God's activity in and through the cross and resurrection of Christ suggests that there is good and evil, that God is at work to bring good out of evil, and that evil is not God's doing.

In monism creation gets both God and people in trouble and God has to do things to offset the effect of it. In dualism, God and an evil force are locked in combat. God is only on one side, a redemptive side.

Either way—monism or dualism—God has to bring good out of evil. Where this evil comes from is the question in both cases, a question weighted with mystery. Whichever is true, *The Wish Giver* suggests that we have to deal with this mystery. We cannot go through life without doing so. The story is a good introduction to this issue for children.

Conversation Starters

■ Why did the Wish Giver warn the children to think carefully about what they wanted?

■ How do you feel about the way the Wish Giver responded to the wishes of the children?

■ What was different about Polly's wish from the other two?

Protection from Danger

DOCTOR DE SOTO
by William Steig
32 pages
(New York: Farrar, Straus, and Giroux, 1982)

In cartoon fashion the author communicates a timely point. A dentist in the form of a mouse outwits a fox who comes to him with both a tooth and a "tummy" ache.

There may be no greater source of disillusionment for children who have been brought up to believe in God's protection than the world in which we live. Television provides a daily attack on faith at this point. The pictures of missing children appear during commercial breaks and on the bulletin boards of grocery stores and post offices. Stories of nursery school teachers assaulting children are themselves an assault. Whether the allegations are true or false, children are made to realize that this is a dangerous world. Survival takes more than passively believing that God will watch out for them.

Coping with danger requires a fresh approach for faith, and the story of Doctor De Soto and his wife can serve to at least stimulate the thoughts of parents, teachers, and children in a more realistic direction. It is a way to open up conversation on this subject that inspires the imagination without frightening the young reader.

The doctor is a dentist. He is also a mouse. However, his practice is not limited to other tiny animals. Indeed, he is especially popular with large animals. Small ones can sit in his chair while he works, but larger ones sit on the floor while he fills a cavity or removes a tooth, working from the appropriate rung on a step ladder. For really large animals his wife helps by operating a hoist that lowers the doctor into the mouth of the patient.

Large animals appreciate him because, being so small, he is by nature gentle and his drill is so tiny they hardly feel it. Yet he gets the job done.

However, knowing the nature of some larger animals, such as cats, a sign hangs outside his office which reads "Cats and other dangerous animals not accepted for treatment." And just to be on the safe side he and his wife both look out the window when the bell rings. Before opening the door they size up the patient on the sidewalk below.

One day a fox in acute molar distress rings for help. At first they point to their sign, but seeing his pain and agony they decide to let him in. Pictures as well as words tell us that the fox—true to his nature—has a pain in his stomach as well as in his tooth. His tooth is indeed killing him but he is also hungry, and with a mouse in his mouth a smile forms on his face suggesting that the thought of a tender morsel is taking shape in his mind.

Sensing this Dr. De Soto places a pole in the mouth of the fox to keep the jaws apart while he and his wife extract the tooth. What challenges their ingenuity, however, is how to protect themselves when the pole is removed. Happily for the dentist and his wife, the fox does not bother them, but that does not relieve their minds of worry because maybe the fox is waiting to "get them" on the next day when a new tooth has to be inserted.

It is at this point in the story that the situation can illustrate to the reader the need and possibility of using one's imagination in being aware of danger and avoiding it. The next day, after inserting the new tooth, Dr. De Soto tells the fox about a mixture he and his wife have that can be applied to teeth and rid their patients of toothaches forever. The fox falls for it, and once the special preparation is applied and he is told to close his mouth, he discovers that he cannot open it again. The special preparation, he is told, will take two days to dry, and then he will be able to open his mouth. The fox leaves, having been outfoxed, or outmoused; his plans to turn Dr. De Soto and his wife into a tasty vittle come to an empty end.

In the animal world the practice of larger animals making meals out of smaller ones seems instinctive. It is built into their relationship. In the human animal world the experience of larger or stronger people harming smaller, weaker ones may not be an instinct but it is presently also a part of what we call life or reality. One day, perhaps, lions and lambs will sit down together, according to the Bible, but in the meantime there is a need for caution in the people population.

The story of Dr. De Soto can also illustrate the tension between danger and humanitarianism, or being kind to animals. From all appearances, a stranger can seem perfectly harmless, even in need of help. But younger children are wise to not yield to the impulse to be of assistance unless they know the person well. Even then it is not foolproof. Abuse and kidnaping can occur within the family because children have little reason to be suspicious of someone they love.

Dr. De Soto is a wise dentist, wise enough to outwit a fox. He gives in to his occupational desire to help someone in need, but he is also old enough and sufficiently street-wise to take care of himself. Smaller children may not be. The story provides the opportunity to talk about this with children. It also provides the opportunity for telling children that in a world such as ours one of the ways God seeks to protect us is to develop within us a need for caution.

Conversation Starters

- Have you ever been in danger? If so, describe what it was like.

- Why did you think it was dangerous?

- What precautions did Dr. De Soto take to avoid danger?

- What might we do when we are in a dangerous situation?

The Power of the Poor

THE BEGGAR QUEEN
by Lloyd Alexander
237 pages
(New York: Dutton, 1984)

While born to a royal family, a princess becomes the queen after being raised among the poor. They place her on the throne, whereupon she eliminates the monarchy and holds a free election.

In 1986, Lloyd Alexander was one of the featured speakers at the International Reading Association's Conference in Philadelphia. During the question and answer period someone asked him why he put so much violence in some of his books, such as *The Beggar Queen.*

He gave two reasons. One, that's the way the world is. The daily news seems preoccupied with it. And secondly, his purpose is to make violence tragic and unappealing.

This book is Part Three of a trilogy. The setting is in the Middle Ages in a country called Westmark. A revolution in a prior volume has placed Mickle, the young daughter of a monarch, on the throne and deposed the power-hungry chief minister—Cabbarus—to neighboring Regia, where he is given lodging on the estate of the Duke of Regia. The two think alike.

Her "title" and that of the book come from having been raised in what some might call the seedy part of town. The beggar queen was raised there to escape the aims of Cabbarus to eliminate all trace of the monarchy. She is street-wise to the point of being able to talk in the jargon of a thief. Because of this background her sympathies lie with the poor, and it is for this reason that the Duke and Cabbarus agree she must go.

Their reasoning Alexander expresses clearly. Since the revolution—the one which placed her on the throne—she seems bent on destroying the aristocracy, "slicing the noble estates into pieces and turning them over to the peasantry." The Duke of Regia sees this as a contagious disease because, "It infects, it spreads. We already have a rash of it."

Consequently, from his own fortune, the Duke supports the effort of Cabbarus to unseat the queen in Westmark, along with her consuls, and put himself in power. He wants to be known as Head of State or King, but until then he settles for something that suggests guidance and service, such as Director. His first directive upon successfully pulling off a surprise takeover of Westmark is to build a huge gallow.

He identifies his motive to be that of clearing the land of corruption, meaning the group of ragamuffins and thieves the Beggar Queen has surrounded herself with. He has support from many landowners and merchants who are overjoyed to see the last of the Beggar Queen.

While the words are not used, it is apparent from the way the characters are described, and especially from the things they do, that this is a story of the age-old struggle between good and evil, except that the definitions do not quite match the ones to which we may be accustomed. There is a tendency for those who are wealthy and in power to view themselves as "good," and anyone who would try to wrest either one from them as "evil." Alexander turns this upside down.

At the same time, he is not naive when it comes to human nature, especially in a war. Good does not come off untainted. For example, during the revolution that successfully placed Mickle on her rightful place on the throne, Theo was capable of bloodshed. After the revolution, all he wants to do is to return to his occupation as an artist and painter.

While the landowners and the merchants think that they have seen the last of the Beggar Queen, with Cabbarus again in power, the truth is that she has been spirited away—once again—for her own safety. The part of the capital city of Marionstat to which she is taken is appropriately called The Shambles. It is the northern edge of the city, a world of cheap wine shops, dicing dens, and flea markets. The queen, returning to such a world, is like a "fish thrown back into water." She is as at home there as in the palace.

The particular place where she is in hiding is a junk shop, a pawnshop, or both. It is run by Ingo, a kind of Robin Hood figure who knows that he will be a thief under the monarchy, the consulate, or now under the directorate. To him one government is the same as the next. "They'll hang us just as high." But for the sake of the Beggar Queen, not her desire to rid Westmark of Cabbarus, he agrees to hide her. At the same time, having been raised as a waif or guttersnipe, it is easy for her to move about disguised as one, as she plans the way to regain her throne and her people. In spite of Ingo's occupation he is drawn to Mickle as are many other people despised and rejected by society. There is something in her they admire or want to protect.

Cabbarus sends his henchmen throughout the land looking for her, unaware that she is right there in Marionstat, in exile as it were, operating her government from a pawnshop. Efforts are made to rid Westmark of Cabbarus through an insurrection led by the same ones who earlier successfully brought off the revolution.

However, the story takes an unexpected turn, when despite all the planning, the insurrection occurs as if by spontaneous combustion among the people. They have had enough of the hangings, being shot on sight, arrested, tortured, etc., and one day when a cart spills over in a street they turn it into a wall between them and the forces of Cabbarus. During the ensuing battle Theo and Mickle, who are sweethearts, are momentarily caught and brought before Cabbarus. However, when Cabbarus is assassinated before their eyes by one of his "trusted" spies, they escape through an abandoned well the Queen knows about, and soon find themselves on the edge of the city. Meanwhile, it is safely secured by the people themselves.

The Beggar Queen remains true to her people. She abdicates the monarchy in favor of a democracy, wherein they are free to exercise their own choice for someone to succeed her. Participatory democracy enters the picture as the story ends.

There are a number of characters in this story whom we have not mentioned, but whom Alexander develops in a truly fascinating manner. He knows human nature well. Indeed, concerning this final volume in the trilogy he writes, "Though eager to take up new adventure in Westmark, I began *The Beggar Queen* reluctantly, fearful of what might happen to characters I had lived with constantly and fondly these several years. But the forces previously set in motion had to work themselves out to their own conclusion, in events both surprising and inevitable."

The Beggar Queen herself comes across as a kind of Christ figure. Raised among the poor and despised, intimately acquainted with their suffering, as was Jesus, she does not lose her love for them, despite being elevated to royalty. Of course, Jesus refused to be used to remove the Romans from power, or to overthrow the Jewish hierarchy. However, if a monarch were to emulate the qualities of Jesus known through his ministry, they would surely resemble those of Mickle.

One of the characters we did not mention has the name Liberation, a name that may remind some of the liberation theologians in Latin America. The conflict there is between those in power and the poor. One also thinks of the Philippines where a woman assumes the presidency when the long-time, corrupt incumbent is forced out of office and the country, due to the power of the people and their allegiance to their own Beggar Queen, Mrs. Aquino. South Africa also enters in between the pages of this story, as one reads about the rising tide of resistance there to the autocractic white leaders who seek to keep the black majority poor and powerless.

There is something or Somebody at work in the midst of oppression bringing courage and leadership to the fore. Viewing Christ as a liberator in such circumstances has theological sanction, and is not untrue to the gospel stories when he spent his life among the poor and disenfranchised members of society.

Conversation Starters

- What are the differences between the "crimes" of the poor and those of the rich?

- Is "spontaneous combustion" an accurate way to describe the uprising of the people in Westmark?

- What parts of this story do you see relating to what is going on in the world today?

- Is it appropriate to identify the Beggar Queen as a Christ figure?

A Peasant Outwits a Czar

THE FOOL OF THE WORLD AND THE FLYING SHIP
retold by Arthur Ransome
48 pages
(New York: Farrar, Straus and Giroux, 1968)

A seemingly naive and helpless son, symbolizing the world's poor, is befriended by a variety of strange individuals. Together they symbolize God's favor. The story is from the time in Russian history before atheism became its official creed.

As a Russian tale this story not only has an enchanting quality, but it also helps one understand something about Russia at a certain time in history. Russia is a land with the Czar on one side, peasants on the other, and very few in between. The story may even go so far as to help one understand how a country like Russia could become atheistic.

The setting is an announcement by the Czar that he will give his daughter in marriage to anyone who can provide him with a flying ship, literally a boat with wings.

A family with three sons immediately responds. Two of the sons are clever, so clever that "they can borrow money without being cheated," a rather unusual definition of cleverness. The third is very simple so he is called "the fool." Even his parents seem to despise him.

All three set off in search of the ship, but the first two, the clever ones, are never heard from again. We might have anticipated this with the word fool appearing in the title of the story. Another clue would be the explanation that "This is a story that shows that God loves simple folk, and turns things to their advantage in the end." This image that the Russians had of God might contribute to atheism as much as to belief.

The young man departs with some crusts of black bread and a flask of water in his sack. He immediately encounters an old man who asks him how he is going to make a flying ship. The fool responds that he does not know but "God knows."

Then the old man says, "Let's eat what God has given." At this point the reader knows this is a story of miracles because the food in the sack turns out to be white rolls, cooked meats, and corn brandy. "You see how God takes care of simple folks" explains the old man.

Then "the fool of the world" is told by the old man to go to the first big tree in the forest, strike it three times with an ax, and then go to sleep on the ground until someone wakes him up. With utmost faith the young man does what he is told, and a flying ship appears.

Our friend, the fool, climbs into his flying ship and sails off toward the Czar's palace. Along the way he meets and invites a number of unusual characters to join him. They prove extremely valuable later on, for upon arriving at the palace he discovers that the Czar is not too happy at the prospect of his daughter marrying a "dirty peasant." Thinking he can get out of his original offer, the Czar assigns the fool a number of what he assumes will be impossible tasks, only to find out that somehow the fool succeeds each time, with the help of his passengers. In the end he wins the Czar's daughter as a prize, and is no longer thought of as the fool.

However, before the fool succeeds we are exposed to what I feel is the main message of the story—the different attitudes between the fool of the world and the Czar over "distinctions in life." The Czar's very position depends on such distinctions, whereas the fool does not even notice them. He has respect not only for himself but for everyone he meets.

Moreover, it is clear from the miraculous things his friends are able to do that the original teller of this tale associates miracles with God and God is indeed at work to "turn things to the advantage" of the simple peasant. There is, in other words, another force in the world besides that of the Czar, one that brings to mind the words of Jesus concerning "Blessed are the meek, for they shall inherit the world." Obviously they could not do that unless a superior power was on their side. God is determined to eliminate distinctions, to work for justice and equality, and it is this that says something about Russia today.

Although the fool may have forgotten his peasant stock, just as present day leaders in Russia may drive around in big cars, that only means—from the story—that they become like the Czar, and if they make distinctions between people, then they become the object of God's eternal, unrelenting efforts to change the situation.

The world is filled with distinctions, some folks calling others "fools," and it takes a strong force to change such attitudes, one that might be termed "divine intervention." However, one could read the Gospel story this way, considering the amount of time Jesus, as God's Son, spent with the poor and despised of the world.

There is little evidence that God's way of working is through out-landish miracles as in this story. God's way seems less obtrusive and more discernible through pressure, the pressure for justice that is at work in history, and in the lives of nations and people. If as in the case of Russia, prior to the revolution there, the church is not on the side of justice, such pressure has no link with faith and God must go about his work unrecognized, unacknowledged. This can be true here in our country as well.

Conversation Starters

- What might have influenced the parents' different views of their own children?

- What results could this have in real life?

- Why is he called the "fool of the world"? How does that description compare with Paul's description of the followers of Jesus in 1 Corinthians 4:10?

- In what way can an emphasis on the miraculous lead to atheism?

When the Bottom Moved the Top

YERTLE THE TURTLE AND OTHER STORIES
by Dr. Seuss
80 pages
(New York: Random House, 1958)

Power and its effect on other people are the twin themes in this allegory that uses turtles to convey the message. The story strikingly illustrates a statement of Jesus concerning those who would be his followers.

It isn't quite true that when you have seen one turtle you have seen them all. Not only do they differ in size, but in this delightful allegory by Dr. Seuss they also differ in their state of mind.

Take Yertle, for example. He looks like other turtles with a shell, legs emerging from the sides, a tail from the back, and a head from the front. However, for reasons not stated, Yertle thinks differently. Some today might say he is a left-brained turtle, the only one in his clan.

Though it doesn't add up, he equates being King with seeing all he can see. All is well in turtle pond until the day that Yertle decides that if he was a little higher up he would not only see more but rule more. The reason may be flimsy but the effect is devastating for the other turtles in the pond.

Yertle has that quirk in his personality that intimidates others. Upon issuing the command, other turtles climb on top of each other. Putting it in Dr. Seuss' rhythmical way, "He made each turtle stand on another one's back, and he piled them all up in a nine-turtle stack."

Upon climbing to the top Yertle sees much more and immediately declares that he is now the ruler of a cow, a mule, and a house. The cow, the mule, and the house do not realize that they have a ruler. It is much like the early "discoverers" of the Americans landing on shore and announcing that the land—as far as they can see—now belongs to

Spain. That it has been there long before they "discovered" it makes no difference. The difference is in their point of view, or self-opinion.

Yertle basks in his royal view all morning until he hears a faint sigh from below. The turtle at the bottom, a fellow named Mack, is experiencing soreness in his back, shoulders and knees and asks, "How long must we stand here, Your Majesty, please?"

Not only does Yertle respond by commanding silence below, but also by ordering more turtles to come and raise his throne. In a fashion that sounds all too much like human history, they obey. Stepping on Mack's head, they climb to the top to give King Yertle more to view and more to rule. The illustrations in this book tell the story. Signs of strain show on the faces of the turtles below as the weight above becomes too heavy to bear while Yertle, being on the top, feels no weight above him at all.

The picture brings to mind a cartoon in the paper of the President of South Africa standing with one foot across the spine of a black worker and commanding him to get to work. The black man is replying that he would be glad to if only the president would "get off his back."

Yertle's view now takes in trees, birds, and bees. "I'm Yertle the Turtle! Oh, marvelous me! For I'm ruler of all that I see." It suggests a strange kind of complex. Perhaps power for power's sake, for all his ruling does is to look all around, everywhere, but down.

The turtles who form the throne are now in great pain—especially Mack. Remember Mack—the one at the bottom? "I know, up on top you are seeing great sights, but down at the bottom we, too, should have rights." Besides they are getting hungry.

King Yertle does not like words about "rights" coming from below. It sounds to him something like a complaint. He quickly lifts his gaze from the misery he is causing to loftier heights, only to spot the moon far above him. Heavens, there is something higher than he.

But before he can implement his desire for more turtles and more height, he is interrupted by Mack who has had enough. Mack burps and that is all it takes to send Yertle head-first into the muddy pond below.

Smiles appear on the faces of all the turtles that are standing on top of each other. At last they are free "as turtles, and maybe all creatures should be," and with that the allegory comes to a close.

A story is an allegory when at various points the action is symbolic of other action. The drive or ambition to reach the top—to be in command—is comparable to what is well known in human society. It even begins, perhaps, in the game children play called "King of the Mountain" in which they try to push the one on top of a rock or hill off so someone else can be on top.

This is the same kind of game that adults engage in when a corporation has a larger office for the executive than for the others who are "employees." At the bottom of the hierarchy are the secretaries, many of whom may have to work in one room. Such a managerial grid has given rise to such terms or phrases as "top brass" or "top dog" or as the head honcho in the sit-com "WKRP in Cincinnati" called "Big Guy."

Yertle the Turtle is a commentary on society which James Wallace Hamilton has portrayed in his book, *The Thunder of Bare Feet*. Hamilton describes what everyone realizes who gives it a moment's thought. Those who covet power reveal a tendency to live on hills that overlook the valleys below. The domestic topography reflects the person's position at work.

Actually in this story we have a children's picture book example of something Jesus said centuries ago to his followers. "The Gentiles lord it over others," he observed, "but this shall not be so among you."

History indicates that the followers of Jesus very often have not taken that idea seriously. However, there is evidence that a whole group of people below who grew up during the sixties have become very aware of their "rights." What is happening in the American workplace is akin to a revolution. Much "burping" is taking place, and one top executive described this change as turning the managerial grid upside down, with the hourly workers on the top and everyone else serving them. Where this is happening the Yertles of industry becomes listeners, cooperators, and colleagues rather than order givers, chief idea persons and warlords.

When we assess what is happening in Latin America and South Africa we realize that the thunder of bare feet is taking place in a literal sense. There is a worldwide revolution going on, and those who read *Yertle the Turtle* to their children are lighting a small fire that is part of this global flame. It is perhaps summed up best by Jesus' words, "The meek shall inherit the earth." God is not a cosmic copy of a corporation president, far above and aloof, but is one with us, among us, trying to move us to a new kind of society and a new kind of leadership, one modeled after Jesus himself.

Conversation Starters

- What in the world got into Yertle the turtle?

- What did he do to the other turtles?

- What or who got into Mack?

- Do you think Yertle realized what he was doing to them? If not, why not?

- How is this story like playing "King of the Mountain"?

- How does this compare with the way Jesus treated people who were poor and without power in the first century?

A Little Bird's Big Influence

THE NIGHTINGALE
by Hans Christian Andersen
24 pages
(New York: Harper, 1965)

This story has overtones of an allegory. Through the beautiful
singing of a plain looking bird God shows love for the poor and
power over the rich and public enemy number one—death.

It is not unusual for someone to cover up the source of a secret by
saying "a little bird told me." What is unusual is how this response may
have originated. The "bird" may very well be the nightingale in this
story, and the one who became heir to the little bird's secret is some
emperor from China's distant past.

Emperors have a reputation for untold wealth and for being more
or less isolated from their "kingdom" by living in a palace. This Chinese
emperor is no exception. His garden is so large the gardener has never
seen the end of it. The emperor is so isolated that the first he knows of
the nightingale on the edge of the garden is when he reads about its
existence in a book written by a scientist.

In one way this is understandable. The people who are privileged
to hear the nightingale sing are not the kind of persons who spend much
time with emperors, or have their ear. The first to hear and report the
singing, for example, is a poor, tired fisherman. When the emperor
reads about this bird's beautiful tones he can not find anyone in the
palace who can confirm it except a helper in his kitchen who takes
scraps of food to her poor, sick mother.

Then, too, the nightingale is very plain, even drab, to look at.
Outwardly there is nothing about it to draw anyone's attention. It is its
singing that earns it an invitation to sing for the emperor in the Great

Presence Chamber, and when it does, it brings tears to the eyes of the monarch. This the nightingale sees as a great reward, for "an emperor's tears have mysterious power."

The singing is so beautiful that even lackeys and chambermaids are quite pleased, and in the story they are most difficult to satisfy. This is less than surprising because lackeys and chambermaids are both on the bottom of the totem pole of servants. They clean up after other people. Their job has few rewards. Satisfaction would hardly be an experience with which they would be familiar.

So the nightingale is the great equalizer in the kingdom. It has the ability to bring together emperors and servants. If this story is an allegory this part brings to mind the Creator's power through a tiny creature able to woo the hearts of all people, a rare achievement, one perhaps only God could bring about.

In a way this story is like a symphony in three parts. Part One shows what "God" can do. Part Two shows what humanity can do. That part occurs when a jeweler sends the emperor a gift, an artificial bird that is the same size as the nightingale, but which is covered with diamonds, rubies, and sapphires. It, too, can sing—one song—when it is wound up. It sounds stilted and mechanical but the Music Master points out that it keeps perfect musical time and looks beautiful. With its delicate internal mechanism it is a tribute to human skill and ingenuity. Besides it is predictable. There are no surprises. It always sings the same song, and after a while everyone can sing it. There is participation. It is like singing some hymns in church.

When the poor fisherman observes how something is lacking though he cannot explain it, the Music Master is moved to write twenty-five books about this rare bird. No one can understand what he writes but all agree that it is profound. Reflecting on this part of the story can cause one to think; what the Creator does speaks for itself and needs no defense.

Unfortunately, one evening the jeweler's bird breaks and so hard is it to repair that it can only be wound up once a year. Unlike the nightingale from the garden it has no inner source of renewal. It just wears out from being wound up too much, and there are no spare parts to be found. In a sense death, decay and rust reveal themselves, the end result of all "things." The nightingale can not be found either.

Part Three in this symphony occurs when the emperor gets sick, so sick that everyone gives him up for dead. Death is his only visitor, and with death comes the emperor's good and bad deeds watching him, and weighing him down.

He cries out for the soothing effect of music. The mechanical bird is there on a pedestal but the emperor is too weak to wind it up, and being alone there is no else around to do it for him.

Suddenly the real nightingale shows up to comfort him. When it sings, death itself is won over and agrees to give up its power over the emperor. Death leaves and the emperor recovers much to the surprise of everyone. When offered a reward the nightingale reminds the emperor of his tears, which already are the reward.

The nightingale agrees to live in the palace, free to come and go, and promises to sing of happy people and of those who suffer, of all that is both good and evil in the kingdom which had been hidden from the emperor. He asks of the emperor only one thing: "Let no one know how you learned all these things. Tell no one that a little bird told you."

God's power shows up again in Part Three of this nightingale symphony. Victory over death is God's gift to us. Grace is included in it, erasing the memory of our "bad deeds." The emperor has already shown his openness to God through his receptivity to the singing of the little bird and as the allegory would have it, the emperor is also open to justice, to hearing about the poor in his kingdom, and helping them.

Music is the medium through which God's grace and power are given in this story, and music does indeed soothe us in worried moments, providing it is soothing music and not harsh, loud noise.

Conversation Starters

- What does the singing of the nightingale stand for in biblical or religious terms?

- Why is it difficult to satisfy lackeys and chambermaids? Why is the little bird able to do this?

- What do the tears of the emperor represent?

- What connection might they have with the nightingale's return?

- Why didn't the little bird want the emperor to tell where his news of the kingdom came from?

- Why didn't Jesus want some of his miracles of healing to be publicized?

Property Was Meant To Be Shared

PETER'S CHAIR
by **Ezra Jack Keats**
34 pages
(New York: Harper, 1967)

A young boy makes room for a baby sister by eventually giving her a piece of "his" property he has used for several years. A child's chair illustrates humanity's indebtedness to the One from whom all blessings flow.

Two themes in this picture book raise questions that go far beyond chairs and things. They even touch the economic order. One issue is: How private is property? The other is: Dare we identify ourselves by what we own, our possessions? Both are symbolized in the story of *Peter's Chair.*

The opening illustration shows Peter on tiptoe putting a toy crocodile on "his" tall building that he has just finished. But the next page shows his dog knocking down this careful bit of construction. Peter does not realize that the noise might wake his new baby sister, but his mother does and she promptly chides Peter.

The next two illustrations reveal what is happening in Peter's house. One by one Peter's things, in this case his cradle and his high chair, are being transformed from blue to pink, from his to hers. It is like seeing the departure of two old friends as far as Peter is concerned. They had become a part of himself, or so he thinks. After all, he has slept and sat in them for several years. A person gets attached to things after using them that long a time.

Then he spots his chair. It is still blue. His parents have not gotten to it yet. This calls for a rescue effort and for running away. Carrying his chair he does both, ending up just outside the front door.

Arranging his chair, a picture of himself when he was a baby, and his toy crocodile on the sidewalk he decides it is time to rest, to sit in his chair for a while. Upon trying to do so he makes an unprecedented discovery. He can not fit into his chair. He is too big and it is too small. He has outgrown his chair.

Just then his mother comes and invites him in for lunch. He pretends not to hear but goes inside and hides, probably hoping to receive some attention by having his mother look for him. When he receives it along with the chance to sit in a grown-up chair next to his father, things seem to come together in his mind. "Daddy, let's paint the little chair pink for Susie."

It is no longer his chair but "the little chair" and he is ready to pass it on to his sister. He has bequeathed his property to her and his identity is still intact.

It is a short story but it reminds me of how some children's clothes used to make "guest" appearances in our home and on our daughter and son during the stage when they grew out of them rather quickly. We had received them from another family who had had the same experience, and we passed them on to still a third family, who in turn shared them with a fourth. From there we lost track of the clothes' travels.

Perhaps because all of the families involved knew what was going on, nobody experienced an identity crisis. Like Peter and his chair, so with the clothes, without realizing it we were discovering that some property is not so private. Possessions are not permanently ours. They are, one might say, on loan.

There are many other examples in life that illustrate this. Garage sales testify to the experience of accumulating things that may have been "ours" for a while, but which lost their attraction and perhaps at that point ceased being ours. At least it is easy to put them out on the lawn for someone else to buy for a quarter when we might have paid five dollars for them originally.

Cars travel the same route. We sell them or trade them in and then someone else sits in the seats we sat in. Sometimes the "parting" is done with a hint of nostalgia as the fun times and memories we had in "our car" are recalled with the departure of the vehicle.

This same experience can happen with houses. Houses are host to numerous guests—renters, owners or people visiting for a time. Most houses outlive us or our stay in them. When a move is planned, our possessions are carefully packed and moved to another house. Sometimes these things rest for years in a trunk or box in the attic or storage area, making one wonder if we really need them.

In the case of elderly persons, sometimes it is necessary to "break up housekeeping" as a prelude to moving to a retirement center, nursing home, or the home of someone else in the family. This means saying "goodbye" to things that have been cherished for years.

So it is that most possessions are shared with many people during the course of a human life. What we call "private property" is not a permanent arrangement and sometimes it isn't our property at all. When a bank holds the mortgage on our house or the loan on our car or other items, the property is really not ours.

Peter's chair, Cathy's car, Mary's house, everybody's money—all are on loan. If there is one owner it is God. Life has a way of spreading "things" around.

Conversation Starters

■ What is your favorite possession?

■ What is meant by the phrase, "You can't take it with you"?

■ How is God the ultimate owner or loaner of all that we have?

■ How is our ownership or loanership different from God's?

God's Love in Human Settings

The Source of Oneness

SARAH, PLAIN AND TALL
by Patricia MacLachlan
58 pages
(New York: Harper, 1985)

A farmer with two children and a woman whose only home has been near the sea are brought together through a newspaper ad. The way each contributes to the union shows genuine love at work in what leads to a family.

If you live on an isolated farm and your wife dies, you might wish to fill the emptiness. And if there are very few potential wives and mothers available in your area, one way to accomplish this is to run an ad in a newspaper. Besides, if your neighbor did it and it turned out fine you have a precedent.

In any event this is what Papa did some time after Mama died. He realized that Anna and Caleb were lonely too. For one thing, they missed the singing. Mama used to sing along with Papa, and with his partner gone, Papa stopped singing too.

What is worse for Anna, who tells the story, is that Mama died after bringing Caleb into this world. Thus, Caleb, too, is a reminder of Mama's death. Indeed, it takes Anna "three whole days to love him."

Papa's ad brings a reply from a woman in Maine named Sarah. Her brother whom she lived with has married and so she feels it is time to move.

Letters are written to Sarah that winter and answers are received to their questions. Yes, she braids hair and makes stew and bread, and no, she does not snore. And in her letter to Papa offering to come in the spring for a month "to see how it is" she adds a P.S. for the children—"Tell them I sing."

The letter simply notes "I will come by train. I will wear a yellow bonnet. I am plain and tall."

When spring arrives along with Sarah, readers receive various clues in the story that things will work out well and that Sarah will stay. The first is that "the dogs loved Sarah first."

In the beginning Papa and Anna are shy but Caleb talks to Sarah "from morning until the light left the sky."

When Sarah speaks of picking some flowers and having them dry upside down so "we can have flowers all winter long," that is clue number two. Caleb, his ears tuned by years of not knowing a mother, hears "winter" and whispers to Anna, "That means Sarah will stay."

When Sarah cuts the hair of both Caleb and Jacob, she puts it outside for the birds to use in making nests. "Later we can look for nests of curls," she adds. Caleb again whispers to Anna, "Sarah said 'later'. Sarah will stay."

The newspaper match seems to be working as everyone in the family wants it to, including, of course, Sarah. She even sings them songs they have never heard.

However, one thing worries the children. Sarah misses the sea which she lived near on the Maine coastline. Efforts to compensate for the absent ocean are made, as when Sarah speaks of sliding down sand dunes. Caleb laments that they have no dunes, but this prompts Papa Jacob to think of the hay stack, and so he says "Yes, we do." Soon all four are outside climbing up and sliding down the straw mound. That evening Sarah reads to them a letter she is sending to her brother. She has written about "sliding down our dune of hay." Both Caleb and Anna pick up the words "our dune" and are overjoyed.

Sarah even teaches the children how to swim in the cow pond. It is like having their own little sea.

One day the family is visited by a neighbor and his wife, Maggie, the other spouse acquired through an ad in the newspaper. Maggie can tell that Sarah is lonely, having gone through this herself. She reveals wisdom of her own when she observes, "There are always things to miss. No matter where you are." Sarah repeats that thought, indicating it means something to her.

Sarah has not shed her assertiveness in this unusual courtship. When a storm gathers in the sky, Papa notes that he has to fix the roof, and Sarah responds, "We will fix the roof." Wearing Jacob's overalls she reveals that she is an excellent carpenter. They get the job done before the squall arrives.

However, by the time they get the sheep and chickens and cows

SARAH, PLAIN AND TALL   75

into the barn it is too late to run to the house, so the whole family spends the night in the barn. Here Jacob puts his arm around Sarah. His shyness is disappearing.

When everything seems to be going so well, a "crisis" comes when Sarah announces that she wants to learn how to drive the wagon. She doesn't say why and the children assume that she wants to leave. Her departure into town causes them to cry. They blame themselves. Part of the trauma is that Anna recalls how a wagon took her mother away and she never came back. Not even Papa knows why Sarah wants to go to town. "She does things her way, you know."

When Sarah does return she assures them she missed them even more than she missed the sea. She had gone to town to buy candles for candlelight suppers, seeds for a garden, a book of songs for family singing, and pencils the color of the sea to use in the picture she is drawing.

Unlike Hollywood and the impressions in America of how courtships work, appearance is not a deterrent here. Love—genuine love— grows in the soil of need, respect, and letting people be themselves.

God is present in this story though not mentioned. There is a postscript referring to the wedding in the church in the spring, but that is as close to "God" as a direct reference is made. Yet, one has the underlying feeling that God is with this family of four, helping them blend together into one. The desire to fill the void comes from all of them. Sometimes Papa Jacob leads the way. At other times Sarah does. But inside and underneath there is the feeling that they are also being led. It is a beautiful story.

Conversation Starters

- What words suggest that Sarah will stay?

- What is more important than appearances in this story?

- What part do the words describing Sarah as "plain and tall" play in the story?

- Why did Sarah want to go alone to town?

- Would you say that God was with this family, gently guiding them through ups and downs? How has God led your family through sad times and happy times?

When Deception Is Appropriate

THE MOVES MAKE THE MAN
by Bruce Brooks
280 pages
(New York: Harper & Row, 1984)

Two boys from different backgrounds in the south learn what it means to be friends and how to deal with truth in the course of their friendship. In a world of suffering, truth may at times be withheld.

The title of this book might give the impression that it is the story about the upward mobility of a white male, passing through one neighborhood to another with his family. Actually it is about a friendship that develops between two boys, Jerome Foxworthy and Bix Rivers, who are opposite in some ways but who also have common needs that draw them together.

On the surface they are as different as night is from day inasmuch as Jerome is black and Bix is white. They both live in Wilmington, North Carolina, but that is like two different worlds, each with its own stereotypes of the other.

Jerome is an excellent basketball player as well as a top notch student, but when the coach grudgingly gives him a "chance" to try out for the junior high team and Jerome makes a shot, the coach remarks, "Harlem Globetrotter stuff . . . I bet you play a lot by yourself . . . What about it, Meadowlark? You play a lot by yourself?"

The white kids see a possible state championship with Jerome on their team, but the coach rigs the tryouts so Jerome fails, and so does the team.

Baseball, on the other hand, in Wilmington is a white boy's game, especially Little League. There are twenty teams, each with different uniforms, stadiums to play in, soda trucks nearby, and Stars of the

Week in every Friday's newspapers. Black youth play among themselves and have none of these advantages.

Despite the stereotypes there are elements of truth woven in, a theme in the story itself. Jerome likes basketball because it fits his personality, and Bix likes baseball because that sport fits his. Each is very good in his sport. Jerome sees that in Bix right from the start, but their paths do not actually cross until they end up the only two boys in a Home Ec class. What comes out is more chemistry than food. Indeed, things start happening when the first assignment is to make a Mock-Apple Pie made from crushed Ritz crackers. They get a kick out of making the best pie in class, but Bix shows his dislike for deception when he realizes that the girls are taking it all seriously, planning to share it with their boy friends as if the pie were a real apple pie.

As they come to know each other they discover that Jerome likes basketball because it defines him with its reverse spins, triple jumps, stutter steps, blind passes. "These are me. The moves make the man. The moves make me." Bix likes baseball because there are no such fake deceptions as there are in basketball. It's all out there in the open for all to see. He is open to the truth whether it be on the athletic field or in a Home Ec class. Indeed, he is obsessed with the truth, for some reason.

Jerome is taking Home Ec to learn how to cook for his two brothers during a time his mother is recuperating from an accident. When he eyes Bix's shiny shoes and wrinkled clothes he concludes that Bix is there for "motherless" reasons also. A mother would keep his clothes pressed, but the one thing a boy could do alone would be to shine his own shoes.

Loners by temperament, they rediscover each other at an abandoned basketball court in the woods. Jerome becomes Bix's mentor in basketball, and he learns fast until it comes to the moves that are necessary in the game. True to form, Bix sees them as deception.

Jerome, the only black student due to desegregation of the white school, is looking for friendship, and wants to talk about this "personality quirk," but finds Bix is uncommunicative. He doesn't even want to discuss the subject of friendship. It is enough for him that they play together. Jerome learns quickly not to probe because eventually Bix does confide in him.

One night Bix tells Jerome that his mother is in a mental hospital.

Jerome also learns that Bix has not seen his mother for months and so he arranges a "one-on-one game" with Bix's stepfather with the prize being that Bix gets to see her if Bix wins.

Bix thinks he can win by straightforward play, no moves, no fakes, but discovers that he cannot. During a lull the stepfather tells Jerome what happened as a result of Bix's "self-righteous truthfulness" in a situation sometime ago. In a moment of anguish Bix's mother had asked him if he loved her—she needed assurance—and thinking of her behavior Bix blurts out "no" which causes the ailing mother to try to kill herself. Bix goes on to win the one-on-one. Because he wants to see his mother so badly he gives in to "moves."

In the hospital Bix makes the biggest move of his life. When his mother does not recognize him, he, rather than embarrass her, pretends that the woman in the next bed is his mother, and then he runs from the room and the hospital never to be seen again. Jerome does receive a postcard from Washington, D.C. once, but it is unsigned. Bix's final move is to start over in another place.

Small children are often brutally frank. They are painfully honest at times, such as the child who saw the emperor wore no clothes and said so. There is a time for honesty, but there is a time to hold back truthfulness for the sake of the other person. As Jesus once said to his disciples, "There are many things I would like to tell you, but you cannot bear them now."

Bix could not talk about his mother's illness or his part in it because he felt guilty. He may, no doubt, have felt he caused it. Seeing his mother frees him from that, and he realizes that she truly is sick. In a sense one truth got him into trouble, but another truth set him free.

Psychotherapists will affirm that denying the truth is a way the human mind has of protecting itself. In affirming his staunch commitment to the truth Bix is at the same time defending his having told his mother how he felt . . . at that precise moment. Most of the time he loved her very much, but it was hard for him to even think of going back to his mother and say he had told a lie because that was how he had felt at the time she asked him the fateful question. In playing basketball with Jerome, Bix found out that deceiving is part of the game, and this helps him accept the idea that deception is appropriate sometimes.

Conversation Starters

- Did Bix understand his mother's condition?

- What did he gain from Jerome to help him cope with his situation?

- Are there ever times when we have to make "moves" to preserve our own sanity?

- In what way did racism force Jerome to learn how to make moves to survive?

- How do you feel about Bix leaving Wilmington and never coming back?

The Case of the Good Father

WHAT MARY JO SHARED
by Janice May Udry
32 pages
(Chicago: Albert Whitman Co., 1968)

> *When Mary Jo finally shared something in class, it was a surprise to her teacher, to her classmates, and to her father. The image of God as "Father" can be shared through this story, whether a father is present or absent in the family.*

"Show and tell" is a frequent feature in elementary grades and Room 201 is no exception. Each morning the teacher allows time for it, and when everyone has contributed except one student, the teacher kindly but persistently asks Mary Jo if she has anything to share that day. At home her father asks her the same question.

To both she answers either "no" or looks down at the floor. It becomes an unhappy moment. It isn't that she does not try to think of something. She tries very hard, but every idea she comes up with someone else has already shared. Twice she comes very close, but fails.

Once is a rainy day when for the first time she has her very own umbrella. She thinks about sharing that but when she arrives in school and enters the coatroom the wall is lined with umbrellas. Sharing such a thing would not be unusual, not at all.

Another time she and her brother capture a grasshopper and put it in a jar with holes at the top enabling it to breathe. The next morning she carries it to school only to find upon arrival that Jimmy has brought a jar with six grasshoppers and has caught them all by himself.

It reaches the point where one night she dreams about what she would share. A small elephant comes into her mind in her fantasy dream but she cannot push it through the classroom door.

One evening, after Mary Jo's father asks if she has shared anything, an unusual thought comes to her mind. She tells her father she is going to share something the next morning and asks if he would be willing to stop by and hear her do it. He is a high school teacher and it just so happens that he does not have an early class the next day.

That morning, holding her father's hand she walks into school and tells the teacher she finally has something to share. With her father sitting in a chair reserved for a guest, she announces that she is sharing him. It catches him and everyone by surprise, but he nods in his friendly way and does not seem alarmed by it.

"He is thirty-six years old and has a wife and three children. His youngest child is me," says Mary Jo.

It is a unique idea that nobody else has thought of but it prompts several others to begin to share things about their fathers. Some ideas are like that. At first they are unique but once they are turned loose others like to comment on the same subject.

The teacher politely discourages the other children from talking about their fathers and returns the spotlight to Mary Jo and her dad. Mary Jo tells of some mischievous things her father had done when he was a little boy and then she says, "and now my father will say a few words."

He gives a little speech. The children clap, and Mary Jo feels good about it. At last she has brought something or someone to share that nobody else has thought of before.

This story does not convey the impression of being an allegory or an analogy, but it has that quality in the "father" serving as a central character. The analogy, with the use of the word "father" to describe the Deity, is a natural one to draw in conversation with children, but it is, in this case, and at this time, not without some qualifications and commentary.

The term "father" for the Deity is sometimes, and not without cause, dismissed as inappropriate because of negative memories or associations that the term may bring to children. This story suggests that there are some positive experiences children have with fathers, and that at least for this class the term has some good connotations.

There is another dimension in this story that deserves comment, one that can be shared with children also. Not all fathers and mothers are present in the home. Sometimes divorce results in the absence of a parent in the family. With so many divorces occurring today many families are experiencing this.

Interestingly enough there is a theological meaning to be seen both in the absence of a parent from a family and in the presence of a parent. One of God's characteristics is that he is unseen, in other words, absent. Parents serve as substitutes for the Unseen Deity until children are able to make the transition from sight to faith in relation to God. This story provides the opportunity to talk about this reality, and for children who are at the age of asking questions, it is a timely opportunity.

Conversation Starters

- How would you describe the relationship between Mary Jo and her father?

- How might she feel about referring to God as "Father"?

- How would a child feel about referring to God as "Father" if the father were no longer a part of the family?

- In what sense is the heavenly Father absent from the human family?

- What does it mean to say our relationship to God is based on faith?

Undertones of Judgment and Mercy

BRIDGE TO TERABITHIA
by Katherine Paterson
128 pages
(New York: Avon Books, 1977)

When a young girl moves nearby, Jess, a farm boy her age, finds that life takes on new, deep meaning. She is a tower of strength even when she unexpectedly dies. Katherine Paterson, a missionary's daughter and a pastor's wife, reveals something of her own faith through the words and events surrounding Jess and his friend, Leslie.

The race is set. Jess has been preparing all summer to be the best in the fifth grade. Then at the last minute, Leslie, a girl who has just moved into the area, asks to participate, and to everybody's chagrin, she wins.

That puts an end to the recess races. However, it is the beginning of a friendship between Jess and Leslie. Because of the race it blossoms amidst the fresh air of mutual respect.

The two are good for each other in several ways. Leslie very much needs a friend, for she wears jeans to school, and even though all the girls can see by their TV what is OK anywhere else, it takes a long time for people in Lark Creek, a rural area, to accept it. Jess, being a boy, does not have this problem.

Then, too, Leslie has never been to church. Her parents are a product of the disenchantment with organized religion that was felt by many young adults from the sixties. In fact, it is because they want to reassess their value structures that they leave a suburban Washington neighborhood with many cultural advantages, and buy a run-down farm not far from Jess' home.

On Easter Sunday Leslie goes with Jess and his family to church.

Jess isn't eager to go. To him it is boring. He is amazed that Leslie joins in the singing. He "drowsily wondered why she bothered." For this fifth grade boy the preacher has a "tricky voice." He would buzz along quite comfortably and then, Bang! He is screaming at you. Because Jess doesn't listen to the words, the sweat running down the preacher's red face seems strangely out of place in the dull sanctuary.

Leslie thought it a great experience. She thinks the story of Jesus dying on the cross after not having done anything to hurt people is beautiful, like the stories of Abraham Lincoln or Socrates. To Jess, a more apt description would be "dreadful." "It's because we're all vile sinners that God made Jesus die."

Leslie has trouble believing this even when Jess says it is in the Bible and his sister adds that if you don't believe the Bible "God will damn you to hell when you die." Leslie just can not believe that, and that is good for Jess to hear.

Their different beliefs may reflect their backgrounds. Fear is much a part of Jess' life. He gets it from the preacher, from his teacher in school who smiles only twice a year—on the first and last day of school—and from his parents. Jess's father does not seem to show much interest in him or share much affection. "Mighty late with the milking, aren't you, son?" is the only thing his father would say to him all evening. Once when he tells his father how much he loves to draw, it prompts the paternal response, "What are they teaching you at that damn school?" Jess' mind is primed for a belief in a judgmental God.

Leslie's parents, on the other hand, are very supportive and loving. She might not have been to church, but she has been exposed to a loving God without realizing it.

It is this background that no doubt gives Leslie the inner strength to befriend Janice Avery, a seventh grade girl with a reputation for being mean to kids who are smaller than she. It happens when Leslie hears sobs coming from the girl's room where Janice often goes to smoke. Entering the room she finds Janice there alone. When she asks what is wrong she learns amidst sobs and curses that Janice's father beats her a lot and that some of Janice's "best friends" are blabbing it around school. Janice even asks Leslie what to do and Leslie's counsel is a big help.

A major part of the story, the one giving rise to the title, is the way the loneliness of Leslie and fears of Jess combine to develop in their minds the need for a "magic place," a kingdom where they can reign as king and queen and not be harassed by others. They find this place on the other side of a nearby creek, reachable by a rope that hangs from a tree limb and swings back and forth across the creek as they wish it to.

They thoroughly enjoy each other's company in this place which they name Terabithia. One fateful day, however, Miss Edmunds, the school music teacher, invites Jess to go with her to an art museum in Washington, and he accepts. Not only has he had a long-standing crush on this teacher, but she is also the only person—besides Leslie—who encourages him in his desire to draw. It was a perfect day.

When Jess returns home that day he finds his family sitting around in mournful silence. The TV is not on. No supper is on the table. Finally one of Jess' sisters blurts out, "Your girl friend's dead." It seems that with Jess in Washington Leslie had gone to Terabithia alone, and when she tried to swing across the creek the rope broke and she fell, hitting her head on a rock. Hearing that news is the way Jess' "perfect" day comes to an end.

The reactions of Jess to this shock are normal and informative for readers of all ages. The first is to deny it. He cannot believe it. This is mixed with his regret for not having invited Leslie to accompany him and the teacher. Later when he goes to her home with his parents he notices a number of people crying, but he does not. A part of him feels important—probably the only person his age whose best friend has died.

When Leslie's father comes over and embraces him, Jess hears him say, "She loved you, you know . . . She told me once that if it weren't for you . . . " His voice breaks but a moment later he adds, "Thank you for being such a wonderful friend to her."

Jess longs to leave the gathering, and when he does, he heads for Terabithia. He throws his paint set into the water and cries, only to find that his own father is there beside him. It is the first father and son talk they have had, and in it Jess' father assures him that God "ain't gonna send any little girl to hell."

Upon returning to school Jess discovers that even the teacher who always seemed cross has a soft spot for Leslie and for him. She provides comfort with the thought that they would never forget Leslie. Jess' inner response to this is to think that maybe someday he'd write the teacher

a letter telling her what a great teacher Leslie thought she was. "Sometimes . . . you need to give people something that's for them, not just
something that makes you feel good giving it."

The story ends with Jess using some lumber from Leslie's back
porch to build a bridge across the creek so his little sister who has been
too small to use the rope can join him in Terabithia as she had often
wanted to do.

The story within this story is that while God can get the reputation
for being angry and uncaring, there is ample evidence that emerges
through people and Scripture that God does care and even comforts us
when conditions become impossible to bear alone. This happens
whether we deserve it or not, for God is a God of grace. As Jesus said,
"I came not to condemn the world but to save it."

Conversation Starters

■ Why did Jess and Leslie like Terabithia so much?

■ What might be reasons why Jess dislikes going to church?

■ What are some reasons Leslie finds it enjoyable and meaningful?

■ What kind of strength do Jess and Leslie give each other?

■ In what ways does this story suggest that life's experiences provide a
  background for what we believe about God and Jesus?

God's Maternal Love

WHERE THE WILD THINGS ARE
by Maurice Sendak
40 pages
(New York: Harper and Row, 1963)

> *Max is sent to bed without supper for being wild. In a bit of fantasy he promptly lives out the part until he longs to go home. The sight and taste of his "still hot" supper brings an end to his adventure and reminds him of his mother's love.*

Most children will conclude from the illustrations on the first few pages of this book that Max is indeed a mischievous boy. Author and illustrator, Maurice Sendak, shows Max wearing his wolf suit and driving a nail into cracking plaster. Then Max chases a dog while brandishing a fork. His next act of mischief is directed at his mother. When she calls him "wild thing," Max says, "I'll eat you up!" For this, he is sent to bed without any supper.

The story suggests that Max takes his mother's description or label of him seriously. He imagines that his room changes into a forest with vines hanging from the ceiling and trees growing out of the floor. Soon his walls become edges of his world, and the ceiling becomes the sky. In his fantasy he sails on a boat "in and out of weeks and almost over a year to where the wild things are."

The main part of the book is the illustrations of these "wild things." Max tames the huge beasts who gnash their terrible teeth and roll their terrible eyes and show their terrible claws and directs them in a wonderfully wild rumpus. Many adults are fearful that these weird monsters will frighten children and cause them to have nightmares, but I have yet to see a child who doesn't delight in them. Maybe it's because Sendak has introduced a twist here that renders them harmless: most of the time smiles appear on the faces of the wild things even though they may have horns growing out of their heads.

A significant aspect of the story is that Max becomes the king, and as king of the wild things, he not only lives up to the name his mother gives him, but the subjects of his kingdom love him. A reader or viewer can get the feeling that for the moment Max is transferring the love he had from his mother prior to being sent to his room without supper to the wild things. Not even in a wild kingdom can one live without love. So Max imagines that they love him even if his mother seems to be angry. They become a temporary maternal substitute.

However, the story has a redemptive ending. Max is drawn from this imaginary kingdom back to his own room only to find that his supper is on the table "and it was still hot." He not only experiences in the land where the wild things are that he wanted to be "where someone loved him best of all," but when he returns to reality he finds evidence of that love there in his very own room. And that is the best of all.

It is hard to read this story and not see some parallels with the famous parable of Jesus about the prodigal son. There is one point of difference in that the biblical son leaves voluntarily, whereas Max is sent to his room where he fantasizes his way out of his "confinement." In a sense both end up "where the wild things are," getting there by different routes.

Both reach a point in their sojourn where they are drawn back home, and in both cases hunger plays a part in it. The striking similarity, however, is that both discover upon returning "home" that they are wanted there and welcomed, one through a father's party given in his son's honor, the other through the warm supper on a table in his bedroom.

There is one other difference between the stories. In the story Jesus told, the father does not "punish" his son in any way; he lets the "world" do that. This happens even though in a sense the son "punishes" the father by leaving him and spending his inheritance foolishly. The parent in Jesus' story no doubt grieves over his son's departure, but he does not have to change his mind about his son. Max's mother, on the other hand, does change her mind from no supper at all to bringing supper to his room.

A message of unmerited, undeserved grace comes through the actions of the parable's father and Max's mother. God's love is quite able to move through both male and female parents. Both reflect God's redeeming presence.

Conversation Starters

- What is Max doing in the opening pictures that is mischievous?

- Why does his fantasy carry him away to where the wild things are?

- Why does he imagine himself to be their king?

- How does Max's mother in the end come through like the father of the prodigal son in Jesus' parable?

- Did you notice that the book begins with smaller illustrations which become mostly full-page? Can you think of any reason for this?

Friendship Is a Built-In Need

CORDUROY
by Don Freeman
32 pages
(New York: Viking Press, 1968)

A store filled with "things" becomes the place where something personal begins to occur, and what begins in the midst of cold- ness and extravagance continues in a setting of warmth and simplicity. A teddy bear finds a home.

Shopping malls and department stores can serve people in a variety of ways. They can be meeting places where strangers feel the presence of other people even if they do not talk to each other. They are places where we can purchase for cash or on credit things we need and do not need. And they can be places where one wonders who buys all the things and then wishes for the money to do so, both in the same breath.

A department store is the scene for this touching children's story, involving a small stuffed brown bear on a shelf and a little girl who would very much like to buy him.

It is love at first sight. Out of all the toys in the toy department, when the eyes of Lisa and Corduroy meet, there is an instant attraction. The only problem is that Lisa's mother has already spent what money she has, and besides, said her mother, "He doesn't look new. He's al- ready lost the button to one of his shoulder straps." With that the two new friends take leave of each other with a feeling of sadness on the part of both of them.

Finally realizing that one of his shoulder strap buttons is missing, Corduroy—suddenly come to life—climbs down from his shelf when the store closes determined to find it. He is looking everywhere when suddenly the floor beneath him starts to move. He looks up into an escalator and observes with a degree of uncertainty, "I think I've always wanted to climb a mountain."

He assumes that the button on a mattress is his, but of course he cannot get it loose without pulling on it. When it gives way he does a back flip and not only knocks over a lamp but arouses the nightwatchman in the process.

The next day he is back on his shelf when Lisa returns with money from her piggy bank to buy him. Carrying him home, she climbs four flights of stairs to her apartment and to her room. The contrast here is clear. There is no escalator and no elevator, only stairs. In her room is a small bed for Lisa and a still smaller one beside it for Corduroy. The scene at home is a far cry from the department store. There is one chair and one chest of drawers. However, it is enough for Corduroy to exclaim, "This must be home," and then to add with confidence, "I know I've always wanted to have a home."

To Lisa he says, "You must be a friend. I've always wanted a friend."

"Me too," she responds and gives him a big hug.

Don Freeman reveals by the above elements in this story that he did not just flip a coin for the setting, or draw straws for it. This story has a message. It has meaning for children to consider as well as adults. The words are not many, but they are chosen with care.

Part of the meaning is that little children who need teddy bears are the luckiest little children in the world. The need for friends is built in, and something is missing in both boys and girls, men and women, until that need is satisfied. The teddy bear in this case is found in the midst of things, but its human qualities are conspicuous and thus so is the need to belong, to not be lonely, and to have a home. Corduroy is like an orphan waiting to be selected by somebody.

Moreover, it would seem fair to say that if the need for a friend is built in, it is a God-given need, reminding us of the comment by St. Augustine, "My heart is restless until it rests in thee." Things such as new chairs, tables, lamps, and beds, by their very nature, are unable to satisfy this God-given need. The most they can do is to create a vague awareness that something is missing, an awareness that is sometimes dealt with by buying more such things.

Thus, when the God-given need is satisfied, there is no doubt in the minds of those involved that this need has been met. It seems to speak for itself, which is one way of describing how it is that an inanimate object such as a teddy bear in a department store acquires the ability to talk and to respond to a live, human person.

Conversation Starters

- Why were Lisa and Corduroy attracted to each other?

- How did Corduroy "know" he had always wanted a home but only "guessed" he had always wanted to live in a castle?

- What is the difference between "know" and "guess"?

- What might God have to do with "knowing"?

Being Human in a Minister's Family

ONE-EYED CAT
by Paula Fox
216 pages
(New York: Bradbury Press, 1984)

This is a mystery story, involving a gun, but no body, no murder, and a happy ending. What makes it a mystery is that the one who pulls the trigger is a minister's son in whom the minister has much pride and trust.

Darkness and the moon help create shadows everywhere. Ned holds the Daisy air rifle that he has been forbidden to use and walks quietly away from the house down near the stable. Suddenly he sees a shadow move and instinctively, before he can think, he lifts the gun to his shoulder, aims and squeezes the trigger. It makes a quick whoosh sound, not loud, and just as quickly he walks to the barn where the shadow moved but it is now gone.

For most persons shooting a gun would be an experience that they would forget. Indeed, they might shoot a gun many times and even at night, but it was different for Ned Wallis. The problem was that Ned's father is the Rev. Wallis, minister of a nearby Congregational church, and it is his feeling that the only thing that comes along with a gun is something dead. So without having fired a shot, the air rifle that Ned had received as a birthday present from his uncle is put up in the attic in a storeroom, until Ned is older.

Ned figured that if he could just fire it once he would get the thought out of his mind. Instead, what happens from that one shot gets hold of his mind and that's all the boy can think about after he sees a cat with only one eye. Ned is certain that the shadow that moved that night was the cat and that, he, Ned, had maimed the cat for life with his one shot.

Several factors combine to prevent Ned from telling anyone at first about the incident. There is his sense of guilt. He is by nature a kind, loving boy. He had intended to shoot only at tin cans. Shooting at something that was alive was an instinct, something that sometimes comes along with guns. So keen is Ned's reverence for life that it bothers him when a friend tries to kill a snake on the way to school.

Ned's concern for others is another factor. Every day he stops by old Mr. Scully's house to help him with chores and visit with him. And later, when Mr. Scully has a stroke and is taken to the hospital, Ned visits the elderly gentleman frequently.

Ned often cares for his ailing mother who suffers from rheumatoid arthritis. He loves her very much and does all he can to make her more comfortable. Living with the thought of having shot the eye out of a cat becomes harder because he feels that if she knew about his terrible deed, it would cause her more pain.

Then there is Mrs. Scallop, the housekeeper. Ned's father has only ten commandments, but Mrs. Scallop has hundreds. She is very hard to talk to because she is either talking incessantly, mostly about how nice a person she is, or is working in sullen silence. There is an air of fear about her that makes her unapproachable.

Another factor is the memory of seeing a face in the attic window on that fateful night. After firing the gun and as he was returning to the house, Ned glanced up at the attic where he would have to replace the gun in its case without anyone seeing him. He thought he saw the face of a person watching him. Then it vanished. He never could figure out who it was or if it were part of his imagination. It was a real mystery to him.

One of the reasons for Ned's keeping the secret to himself for many months is his father's trust in him. When Rev. Wallis put the gun in the attic he did not hide it. It was in plain sight, because his father trusted Ned. That is what is so hard—to reveal having betrayed that trust.

But the main reason is perhaps pride. It comes out in several ways in the story, but never so dramatically as when Ned inquires what a forthcoming sermon is to be about. The father quotes a text from Paul's Letter to the Philippians: "Do all things without grumbling or questioning that you may be blameless and innocent . . . " He adds, "As you do them, my Ned," because he was so proud of his son.

The father notices his son's care for old Mr. Scully and his concern for his mother, and is indeed justifiably proud of his son. But this only serves to erect a wall between Ned and his father as far as Ned's telling him about the one-eyed cat. Actually it isn't that he is afraid of his father. Even had he told him it would probably have prompted no more than a grimace from his father, but it is what Ned feels would be a destroying of the father's pride in him that gets in the way.

Halfway through the story there are a couple of things that emerge that make a little hole in the wall. One is when Ned learns that his mother isn't necessarily like his father. She agrees that Mrs. Scallop, the housekeeper, is practically impossible, whereas the father always makes excuses for her. The other is that Ned, as if to test his father, mentions a time years before when he took one of the small communion glasses and kept it in a box of treasures. He learns not only that his dad knew about it but had purposely not said anything in rebuke or made him give it back. There is a forgiving side to his father after all. Actually, had Ned thought about it more, he could have known this from the patience his father shows toward Mrs. Scallop day after day.

Eventually, on two occasions Ned tells what happened that night with the gun. One is when old Mr. Scully is dying in the nursing home and can no longer talk. After Ned admits it was he who shot the cat, the old man moves his hand over Ned's and applies feeble pressure to it. Ned doesn't know what the gesture means, but he feels as if his old friend was trying to comfort him.

The other time is shortly after his mother receives some medication that enables her to walk about again. One night when Ned is unable to sleep he goes for a walk only to have someone follow him. It is his mother. She too is up and about. The two of them sit and talk, and it is then that he admits shooting at the cat. It is also then that she admits having seen him from the window that night, but she didn't know what he was carrying. She has not really thought much about it, since her son often got up and walked about when he could not sleep.

Ned tells his mother because he learns through her that she is in a sense more human than his father. It happens once when she makes an excuse about being thirsty just to get Mrs. Scallop out of the room, and then she admits to Ned, "I'm not good like your father. Sometimes I tell fibs." Fibbing is what Ned has been doing for months. Whenever the conversation gets to the point where he feels like telling about the cat, he makes up some excuse to leave the room, so he won't have to say more.

The story ends on a happy note, but it also contains a message that is more serious. Ned's mother tells Ned that she once left his father because "I was afraid of your father's goodness." Despite the fact that ministers are human, they do have this image sometimes. This may be why Mrs. Scallop is always telling people how nice a person she is, as if she is trying to convince herself of her goodness in the house of the pastor. The image can come from appearances in the church building where most folks see the pastor. Ned observes how his father is "stately and slow" in church, as dignified as the organ music. At home his voice sounds "real" but in church it is different. It is this difference that shapes the image many folks have of a minister, even the folks who happen to be the minister's spouse and children.

Conversation Starters

- Why didn't Ned tell anyone about the one-eyed cat?

- How does real life become part of the household in the home of the Rev. Wallis and his family?

- Why doesn't Ned want to take a trip with his uncle during Christmas vacation?

- What might contribute to Mrs. Scallop's sullenness?

- What makes Rev. Wallis talk and act differently in his kitchen than when he is in church conducting a service?

Being Punished Unfairly

THE WHIPPING BOY
by Sid Fleischman
90 pages
(New York: Greenwillow Books, 1986)

> *Some royal households of past centuries used an orphan from the street to suffer the punishment due a misbehaving prince. In this story the prince experiences a change of heart from watching someone receive his punishment.*

Prince Brat tied the powdered wigs of the king's guests to the backs of their chairs and then hid behind a footman. When the wigs came flying off as the guests stood up to toast the king, the prince thought it was hilarious. Not so hilarious, however, was the king's response: "Fetch the whipping boy." Since it was forbidden to spank, thrash, cuff, smack, or whip the heir to the throne, a street-wise orphan had the honor of living in the palace and serving as a punishment substitute. He took his twenty whacks without a whimper, which in itself sometimes irritated the prince.

Jemmy-From-The-Streets even got it when the prince refused to learn how to read and write. "Someone else can do it for me," the prince would declare. And so the prince learned nothing while the whipping boy learned to read, write and do sums.

Finding palace life boring, the prince decides to run away and take Jemmy with him. Outside the palace in dense fog Jemmy plans to escape just as two highwaymen, Hold-Your-Nose Billy and Cutwater, appear. Discovering that one of the boys is the prince, the two outlaws realize they have a royal treasure right in front of them. However, when they learn that the prince can't even sign his name to a ransom note, but that the whipping boy can, they conclude that the two boys have reversed roles.

Jemmy's claim to be the prince—to protect the real prince—is met at first with scoffing from the ruler-to-be. The outlaws are confused. Jemmy talks them into sending the prince back to the palace with the note, but the prince refuses to go. "He has sand for brains," thinks Jemmy, because this is a perfect chance for him to escape. Jemmy finally talks the kidnapers into sending the royal horse back with the note. A horse always knows the way home.

The two boys escape at this point in the story and the prince begins to fancy the life of an urchin. He can get dirty for a change. Jemmy resolves to leave the prince as soon as he can and return to the city where he can hide out in the sewers and make money catching and selling rats.

In helping an old man who was hauling potatoes get out of the mud, they hitch a ride back to the city, only to be caught by the two thieves once again, who, by this time, are very angry. The ransom note backfired; it was all jibberish, but since they were unable to read they did not know that. They only know they did not get a cent. They decide to beat the whipping boy—the prince—and do, and the prince doesn't utter a whimper. Jemmy had often dreamt of the prince being whipped, but now when it happened, it didn't seem as satisfying. He feels sorry for the naive royal son, or is he beginning to like him as a friend?

Again they escape and finally the two of them reach the city, where in a crowd the prince hears people refer to him as Prince Brat, and how they dread the time when he will become king. He has never known his nickname before or how people feel about him. He begins to have some remorse for his behavior.

In the crowd they hear that the king is offering a reward for the whipping boy, who it is believed sold the prince to gypsies. Jemmy decides to escape by heading for the darkness of the sewer. Not knowing what else to do, but not wanting to go back to the palace, the prince tags along.

In the dark, rat-infested sewer the prince learns to trust Jemmy, and Jemmy begins to trust the prince who, disliking the sewer even more, decides to return to the palace. Jemmy realizes he doesn't like the sewer anymore either, now that he knows how to read and write. We will leave the nature of the welcome and what happens at the palace to the reader except for a hint.

This story illustrates that watching someone else take the punishment we deserve can wear thin. It redeems Prince Brat from arrogance and meanness. However, as the story implies, Prince Brat's callousness to the punishment meted out to Jemmy is but a reflection of the king's own callousness. He, too, is arrogant and insensitive.

That this royal practice has ceased is a tribute to the redeeming power of compassion and contrition, not wrath or pride. The ending of the story—just to provide that hint—shows the power of love and joy, that such are infinitely more satisfying.

Conversation Starters

- Have you ever been punished unfairly?

- In what way is Jemmy a Christ figure?

- What changes the heart of the prince?

- Why does Jemmy take the place of the prince when they meet the two thieves?

- What evidence of friendship occurs in the story?